Systems

Volume 8

Using Systems Thinking to Solve Real-World Problems

Volume 5
Parcours au Pays des Systèmes
Harold "Bud" Lawson. traduit de l'anglais par Brigitte Daniel-Allegro

Volume 6
Architecting Systems. Concepts, Principles and Practice
Hillary Sillitto

Volume 7
Software Engineering in the Systems Context
Ivar Jacobson and Harold "Bud" Lawson, eds.

Volume 8
Using Systems Thinking to Solve Real-World Problems
Jamie P. Monat and Thomas F. Gannon

Using Systems Thinking to Solve Real-World Problems

Jamie P. Monat

and

Thomas F. Gannon

Systems Engineering Program
Worcester Polytechnic Institute
100 Institute Road
Worcester, MA 01609

ISBN 978-1-84890-235-0

College Publications
Scientific Director: Dov Gabbay
Managing Director: Jane Spurr

http://www.collegepublications.co.uk

Printed by printondemand-worldwide.com

The Systems series publishes books related to Systems Science, Systems Thinking, Systems Engineering and Software Engineering that address trans-disciplinary Frontiers, Practice and Education

Systems Science having its contemporary roots in the first half of the 20th century is today made up of a diversity of approaches that have entered different fields of investigation. Systems Science explores how common features manifest in natural and social systems of varying complexity in order to provide scientific foundations for describing, understanding and designing systems.

Systems Thinking has grown during the latter part of the 20th century into highly useful discipline independent methods, languages and practices. Systems Thinking focuses upon applying concepts, principles, and paradigms in the analysis of the holistic structural and behavioral properties of complex systems – in particular the patterns of relationships that arise in the interactions of multiple systems.

Systems and Software Engineering. Systems Engineering has gained momentum during the latter part of the 20th century and has led to engineering related practices and standards that can be used in the life cycle management of complex systems. Software Engineering has continued to grow in importance as the software content of most complex systems has steadily increased and in many cases have become the dominant elements. Both Systems and Software Engineering focus upon transforming the need for a system into products and services that meet the need in an effective, reliable and cost effective manner. While there are similarities between Systems and Software Engineering, the unique properties of software often requires special expertise and approaches to life cycle management.

Systems Science, Systems Thinking, as well as Systems and Software Engineering can, and need to, be considered complementary in establishing the capability to individually and collectively "think" and "act" in terms of systems in order to face the complex challenges of modern systems.

This series is a cooperative enterprise between College Publications, the School of Systems and Enterprises at Stevens Institute of Technology and the Bertalanffy Centre for the Study of Systems Science (BCSSS).

For further information concerning the Systems Series see
http://www.collegepublications.co.uk/systems/

Table of Contents

Preface

There are many articles and books available on Systems Thinking. Some even provide suggested procedures for using Systems Thinking to solve problems (Bellinger, 2004c; Checkland, 1981; Elmansy, 2017; Goodman & Karash, 1995; Maani and Cavana, 2007). But these are either dated, superficial, or missing important tools. None provides a current, complete, succinct yet detailed step-by step methodology for attacking real-world systems problems. Indeed, at the 26th annual INCOSE International Symposium in Edinburgh in 2016, after a panel discussion on Systems Thinking Applications, an audience member stood up and asked, "Well, if I want to apply Systems Thinking at my own company, how do I go about it?" We realized then that, barring hiring a consultant, there was no good current methodology to be followed by the layperson. This book is an attempt to address this need.

Some have complained that such a book represents reductionist thinking and is thus self-contradictory. But we disagree: methodology is not the same as reductionism. Indeed, all practitioners of Systems Thinking need to understand how to start and the steps to follow along the way when using systems thinking to address an issue. As an analogy, there are many different ways to build a house, but they all start with a foundation and build from there, and the builders must know how to use the tools.

We hope that this handbook provides the reader with a logical, practical, step-by-step approach to using Systems Thinking to solve real-world problems.

1

I. What Is Systems Thinking?

→A perspective, a language, and a set of tools.

The Systems Thinking Perspective

Systems thinking focuses on the relationships among system components and the interactions of the system with its environment, as opposed to focusing on the components themselves. It is holistic (integrative) thinking instead of analytic (dissective) thinking. Over the last several centuries, the scientific method has taught us to decompose complex situations into smaller and smaller pieces to understand them: this is reductionist or dissective thinking. While this has provided us with the benefit of dealing with complex situations, it also ignores the relationships among system components. Those relationships typically dominate the behavior of systems. Systems thinking requires that we study systems holistically, which involves both spatial and temporal dimensions, as shown in Figure I-1.

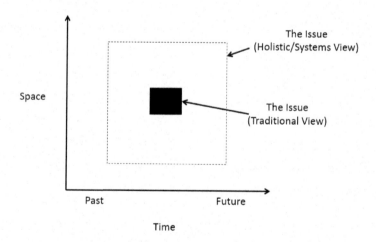

Figure I-1. Systems Thinking versus Traditional Views

Although the space dimension is sometimes easier to grasp than the time dimension, systems thinking requires that we ask: What attitudes and circumstances led to this point? What behavior patterns and actions led to this point? What are the likely attitudes, patterns and actions going forward? What are the probable reactions of others, such as my allies, enemies, competitors, neutral 3rd parties, and the environment? Systems thinking not only requires an understanding of the past, but also a vision of the future.

Systems are also dynamic and are constantly subject to various forces and feedback mechanisms. Some of those forces and mechanisms are stabilizing and some are reinforcing or de-stabilizing. If a system has feedback loops with delays, the system may oscillate, and that behavior is often counter-intuitive. Some examples include checking account balances, employee attrition, the stock market, predator-prey populations, and a swinging pendulum. System dynamics and system dynamics modeling are used to help understand the behavior of systems over time, identify the driving variables so that system behavior may be positively impacted, and predict future states.

Systems thinking is not a substitute for either statistical or reductionist (analytic) thinking; it complements them, as shown in Figure I-2:

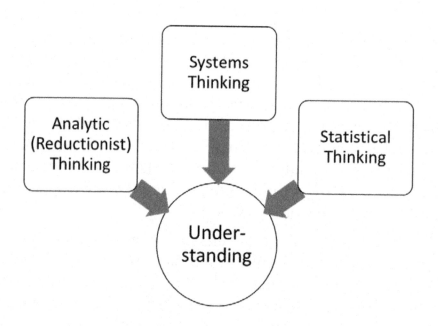

Figure I-2. Systems Thinking Complements Analytic and
Statistical Thinking (Monat and Gannon, 2015a)

Systems thinking deals with **organized complexity.**
Statistical thinking deals with **unorganized complexity**
using statistical mechanics and similar tools dealing with
large numbers of unstructured elements. Analytic thinking
deals with **organized simplicity** using the laws of physics or
mechanics:

Table I-I. Complexity versus Organization

Analytic (Dissective) Thinking   Systems Thinking

	Simple	Complex (Can't be understood using analytical methods alone)
Organized (show structure)	• Crystals • Simple Machines	Display hierarchies, feedback loops, self-organization, emergence, interdependencies, e.g.: • Biological Systems • Electro-mechanical systems • Social systems • Cities • Human Body • Economic Systems
Disorganized (random)	•Bowl of Fruit •Tools in a Tool Box	Many elements; chaotic; statistical mechanics, e.g.: • Gas molecules • Sand on the Beach

Statistical Thinking

All three approaches provide different but complementary perspectives on gaining an understanding of the world around us, but Systems Thinking is most useful for understanding the behavior of systems.

The Systems Thinking Language

The language of Systems Thinking includes a number of key terms such as holism, the Iceberg Model, events, patterns, systemic structures, mental models, self-organization, emergence, complexity, feedback, system dynamics, and unintended consequences. Additional terms include causal loop diagrams and stock-and-flow diagrams which provide effective means for communicating system components and relationships. Monat and Gannon (2015a) provide a concise summary of systems thinking terms.

II. Overall Approach to Using Systems Thinking to Solve Real-World Problems

There are lots of different ways to use Systems Thinking. Here we present a generic approach that has proven useful. Note that the sequence of steps is just a suggestion and certain problems may require skipping or re-ordering steps.

Here is the recommended sequence of steps:

Step 1. Develop and articulate a problem statement.
Step 2. Identify and delimit the system.
Step 3. Identify the Events and Patterns.
Step 4. Discover the Structures.
Step 5. Discover the Mental Models.
Step 6. Identify and Address Archetypes.
Step 7. Model (if appropriate).
Step 8. Determine the systemic root cause(s).
Step 9. Make recommendations.
Step 10. Assess Improvement.

Details follow; note that substantial *research* will be required for most steps.

Step 1. **Develop and articulate a problem statement**. This is often harder than it sounds. We recommend involving all vested parties to reach consensus. The problem statement should be concise but complete. It should not include proposed solutions or recommended courses of action. For example, "The existing order entry system needs to be revised" should be replaced with "Our current order entry system does not serve our customers well. It requires too much effort, too much time, and makes it difficult for

7

customers to change or update orders or to track their orders." Another example: "Our HR department is doing a terrible job" would be better worded as "Our company is having trouble identifying, acquiring, and retaining top talent, as evidenced by high voluntary turnover, lack of new products, and low morale."

Step 2. **Identify and delimit the system**. Tools: Block Diagram, Table, Organizational Chart, Causal Loop Diagrams (CLDs). Defining and bounding the system are important. Define it too narrowly and you will not capture the system characteristics. Define it too broadly and it will take forever to reach a solution. Block diagrams, tables listing what's in and what's out, Causal Loop Diagrams, organizational charts, and flow diagrams are excellent for this task. For large systems, it is sometimes tempting to define the system as (for example) "all of Europe" or "the entire socio-political-economic structure of the country" or "the entire corporation." This delimitation is not especially useful however, and in such situations it is often more useful to identify the key factions or groups comprising the system. For example, defining the corporate system as "Sales, Marketing, Operations, Manufacturing, R & D, Customers, Suppliers, Stockholders, products, services, and physical facilities" may be more useful than defining it as "the entire corporation."

Step 3. **Identify the Events and Patterns**. Tools: Iceberg Model, Behavior-Over-Tome (BOT) Graphs. Behavior-Over-Time graphs help us to identify patterns. The Iceberg Model assists with this and in determining the causes of those patterns.

Step 4. **Discover the Structures**. Tools: Iceberg Model, Causal Loop Diagrams, Stock-and-Flow diagrams, simple verbal descriptions. Systemic structures are the interlocking stocks, flows, and feedback loops, specifically the organizational hierarchy; rules and procedures; authorities and approval levels; and incentives, compensation, goals, and metrics. CLDs and stock-and-flow diagrams help visualize the interactions among system components and the feedback mechanisms that are present. The Iceberg Model helps determine which mental models cause those structures and how the structures yield patterns and events.

Step 5. **Discover the Mental Models**. Tools: Iceberg Model. Mental Models are often the underlying forces that result in the structures characteristic of human-designed systems. The Iceberg Model is a great tool for discovering these.

Step 6. **Identify and Address Archetypes**. In systems thinking, archetypes are negative structures that are common in many situations, environments, and organizations. Fortunately, there are some good solutions available once the archetype is identified.

Step 7. **Model (if appropriate)**. Tools: Stock-and-Flow Diagrams, System Dynamics software. Modeling system dynamics can be useful to help understand the dynamic relationships among system components and the behavior of systems over time. It can also help identify system leverage points so that improvements can be made. Modeling is not necessary for every system, however.

Step 7a. Develop the Model. Use stock-and-flow diagrams and software (such as isee System's "Stella Architect" or Ventana Systems's "Vensim") to develop a dynamic model.

Step 7b. Validate the Model. Run the model to see if it accurately reproduces real systemic behavior. This is sometimes hard to do for large, complicated socio-economic systems.

Step 7c. Identify Leverage Points. Identify those parameters in the system that have a significant impact on systemic performance. These are your control points.

Step 7d. Optimize. Vary the values of the leverage points to determine optimum values.

Step 8. **Determine the Systemic Root Cause(s).** Root cause analysis is a useful tool. In systems thinking, however, it is pushed beyond conventional analysis to determine the underlying root cause *system* or *systems*. Organizational culture and environment are often the problem.

Step 9. **Make recommendations**.

Step 10. **Assess Improvement**.

The sequence described above is a good, but not essential, path to address systems issues. Sometimes archetypes are apparent at the outset; other times behavior over time is clear and is a good starting point. Use the sequence that makes most sense. Sometimes dynamic modeling is essential; other times excellent conclusions may be drawn from only a causal loop diagram.

Before we demonstrate this approach with real-world examples, it makes sense to explain each of the tools independently, in some detail.

III.   The Tools

There are several excellent systems thinking tools. View these as an arsenal of potential weapons that you should use as appropriate. You do not need to use all the tools for every situation. Instead you should select the best tool or tools in each case.

The Tools: The Iceberg Model

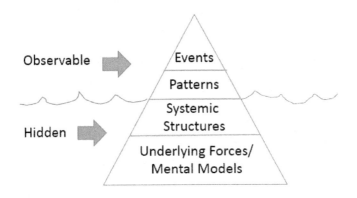

Figure III-1. The Iceberg Model (Monat and Gannon, 2015a)

The Iceberg Model argues that mental models and systemic structures, which are often hidden, give rise to events and patterns (often in the form of behaviors) that can be observed. Examples of Mental Models include "Incentive compensation increases productivity," "Work hard and you will succeed," and "A college education is essential for getting a good job." Examples of systemic structures include commission structures; organizational hierarchies; social hierarchies; rules and procedures; authorities and approval levels; incentives, compensation, goals, and metrics; and feedback loops and delays in the system. Often these mental models and resulting structures yield *desired* events and patterns, as when all sales representatives work hard to generate sales because their compensation is driven by this behavior. On the other hand, sometimes the mental models and concomitant structures yield *unintended consequences* as when a sales representative "steals" a sale from another sales rep on the same team or when a college education results in so much debt that the student can never recover.

One fundamental concept in systems thinking is that different people in the same structure will produce similar results. Deming (1982) has observed that these structures (as established by management) cause 85% of all problems; not the people! To understand behaviors (events and patterns), one must first identify and understand the systemic structures and underlying mental models that yield them.

An excellent first step in figuring out how a system works is to draw a Causal Loop Diagram or CLD. Causal Loop Diagrams show how the various system components inter-relate. They are especially helpful in showing reinforcing and balancing feedback processes, which are present in most systems (and are often ignored in linear thinking analyses). Feedback loops are sometimes obvious (as is the positive (reinforcing) feedback mechanism in interest compounding in a bank account or in the negative (stabilizing) feedback mechanism in a home thermostat. [Note that "positive" does not necessarily mean "good" and "negative" does not mean "bad;" positive means that the feedback reinforces or adds to the causative factor and negative means that it acts against the driving force.] On the other hand, sometimes the feedback loops are not so obvious (as in the case of financial bailouts reinforcing bad business decisions). CLDs can become complicated as various cause-and-effect relationships are identified and depicted.

Kim (1999) and Meadows (2008) present some excellent examples of CLDs, one of which is shown in Figure III-2.

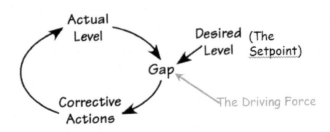

Figure III-2. Generic Causal Loop Diagram (adapted from Kim, 1999)

The difference between the desired level and the actual level represents a gap which drives corrective actions.

Example

You love beer! In fact, you are addicted to it: you have 2-3 beers every day after work, to relieve stress. You are acutely aware of how much beer is remaining in the refrigerator at any time, since you check it hourly---when the level of beer gets low, you get anxious, and the lower the beer, the higher the anxiety. If you were to go 24 hours without beer, you would start to sweat, develop headaches, and grow angry and ill-tempered. Your spouse/significant other does all the food and beverage shopping for the household. You'd like to analyze this situation to see if you can improve the system and thereby improve your relationship with your spouse, as well as reduce your own anxiety.

1. Please construct a causal loop diagram depicting this system.

2. How does this system affect the relationship between you and your spouse?

3. What could you do to improve it?

You start by constructing the following Causal Loop Diagram:

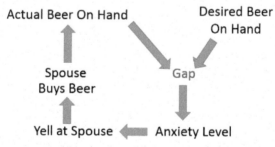

Figure III-3. First Cut at Beer CLD

But then you realize that you have left out some emotional feedback loops, so you revise the diagram:

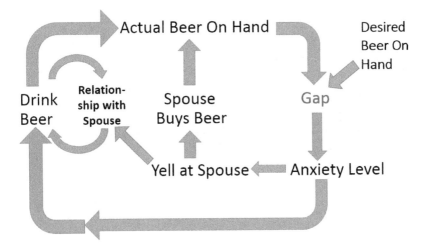

Figure III-4. Second Attempt at Beer CLD

And this diagram is a much more accurate depiction of the system. This illuminating causal loop diagram reveals a structure that is very common in work and in life: there is something that you want or need, but someone or something else has control over it; you can acquire what you want only by influencing the entity with control (think beer as above; supplies that you need that purchasing orders; data that you need that are supplied by the IT department).

There are several solutions to this system. First and best: eliminate the middle-man if possible. In the beer case, there is no reason that you should not purchase the beer yourself, which would improve the relationship with your spouse and relieve your anxiety. This is a fundamental change in the systemic structure. If that is not possible, another solution would be the establishment of agreed-upon re-order quantities and inventory check frequencies. In this case, the inventory level is checked frequently enough so that you would be comfortable, and beer is restocked automatically when the inventory falls below some pre-established value.

Note that Causal Loop Diagrams represent the *only* systems thinking tool required to address and improve this system.

Behavior-Over-Time graphs are time plots of relevant system variables. They are useful in illustrating patterns of system behavior as a first step in developing an understanding of that behavior. These graphs are also useful in gaining an understanding of how system variables inter-relate. As shown in Figure III-5, Behavior-Over-Time graphs can provide insights into common patterns of behavior, such as stabilizing, balancing, reinforcing, positive and negative feedback loops, as well as oscillations and ineffective or absent feedback loops. In general:

- Time plots that converge indicate stabilizing, balancing, or negative feedback loops

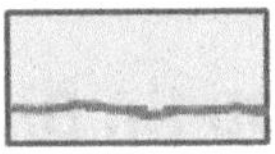

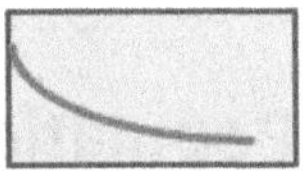

- Time plots that diverge over time indicate reinforcing or positive feedback loops

- Time plots that neither converge nor diverge indicate ineffective or absent feedback loops

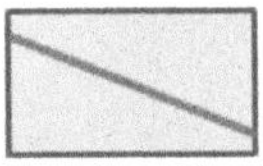

- Time plots that oscillate indicate feedback loops with delays

Figure III-5. Common BOT Graphs

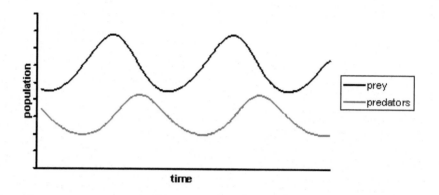

Figure III-6. Predator-Prey Curve

For example, Figure III-6 shows a predator-prey population curve that oscillates, indicating feedback loops with delays. This represents a good starting point for investigating the nature of those feedback loops using a causal loop diagram and dynamic modeling.

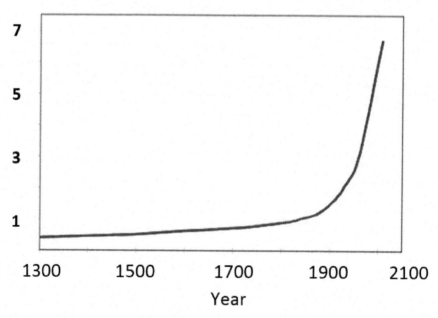

Figure III-7. Population Growth Curve.

In Figure III-7, a population curve shows exponential growth over time, indicating a positive (reinforcing) feedback loop. The next step would be to determine the nature and causes of that feedback loop, again using a causal loop diagram with dynamic modeling.

Figure III-8. Basic Stock-and-Flow Diagram

In order to execute dynamic modeling of systems (which is useful for understanding systemic behavior over time) we must start with stock-and-flow diagrams. These are often converted from Causal Loop Diagrams (CLDs). Gene Bellinger (2004b) provides handy instructions for converting CLDs into stock-and-flow diagrams.

In systems, some quantities are stored while others flow. These may be real physical quantities such as dollars, volume of water, number of customers, or number of cabbages in a field. They may also be non-physical quantities such as love, anger, greed, or other emotions. Stores or accumulations of these items are called "stocks". Stocks increase or decrease as quantities flow into or out of them. Like causal loop diagrams, stock-and-flow diagrams are helpful in understanding systemic behavior.

Here is a first attempt at a beer stock and flow diagram corresponding to the beer causal loop diagram (CLD) shown earlier in Figure III-3:

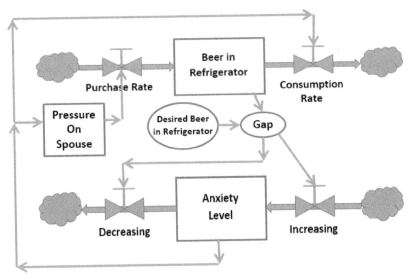

Figure III-9. First Attempt at Beer Stock-and-Flow Diagram

But as for the CLD, we have omitted some relationship-based stocks and flows:

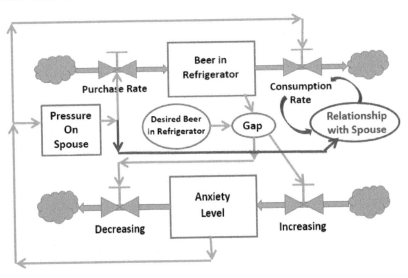

Figure III-10. Revised Beer Stock-and-Flow Diagram

This stock-and-flow diagram depicts all the important stocks and flows in this system, including emotions and relationships. It could now be used to develop a dynamic model of the beer system.

System Dynamics is the study and analysis of non-linear behavior of complex systems over time using stocks, flows, feedback loops, and time delays. The behavior of a complex system is often non-intuitive and difficult to understand. Modeling the system helps one understand why the system (company/individual/department) behaves the way it does. Modeling also helps identify control points and how one can influence system behavior. A number of software packages are available for system dynamics modeling, including Stella Architect and iThink from isee Systems, Vensim from Ventana Systems, and Powersim from Powersim AS.

A comprehensive list of system dynamics modeling tools can be found at http://en.wikipedia.org/wiki/List_of_system_dynamics_software.

In their most basic form, System Dynamic models are typically *control volume analyses*: an initial quantity or stock increases over time due to an inflow and decreases due to an outflow:

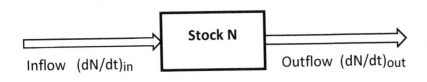

Figure III-11. Control Volume Analysis

Here t is time and dN/dT represents the instantaneous change in N with respect to time. If N_0 represents the initial value of the stock, then this model yields the equation

$$N = N_0 + [(dN/dt)_{in} - (dN/dt)_{out}]\Delta t$$

which the software uses to calculate the population N as the simulation marches forward in time increments Δt.

To model the dynamics of a system, one typically starts with a causal loop diagram and then translates this into a stock and flow diagram. Links among stocks and flows are then added, and initial values are established for each stock. Next, algebraic equations are developed to represent the inflows into and outflows from the stocks. The simulation is then run and debugged. The results are typically plotted in behavior-over-time plots which must then be compared with reality to validate the model. Once validated, control points may be identified and experiments conducted to see how to best influence the system. Excellent, detailed instructions on how to model are provided by Barry Richmond (Richmond, 2004).

For example, an Asian wildlife biologist is in charge of introducing snow leopards (*Panthera uncia*), an endangered species, to a new habitat in the mountains of Inner Mongolia (Jackson and Ale, 2009). She'd like to know how many individuals N_0 she should introduce as the seed population, how long the seed population will require to grow, and if it will reach a steady-state value. She develops the following stock-and-flow diagram:

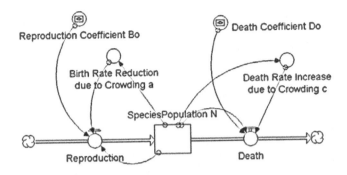

Figure III-12. Endangered Species Reintroduction

And, after reviewing population growth research, she develops the following equations for inflow (reproduction) and outflow (death):

Species Reproduction Rate = $(B_0-aN)N$ where N is the number of individuals present, B_0 is the reproduction rate coefficient (in number of offspring born per parent per year) when N is small, and a is the birth rate reduction due to crowding.

Species Death Rate = $(D_0+cN)N$ where D_0 is the death rate coefficient (in % of the population that die each year) when N is small and c is the increase in the death rate due to crowding.

The *carrying capacity* C of the region may be expressed as $C = (B_0-D_0)/(a+c)$ and is in units of number of individuals.

For this particular species and geography, she estimates $B_0 = 2$, $D_0 = .5$, and a $= c = .00015$ (which yields a carrying capacity C $= 5,000$ individuals). She decides to experiment with various seed populations N_0 ranging from 50 to 500, realizing that the individuals of this species are very rare and hard to acquire. She develops the model using isee's Stella

25

Architect software and produces the following plot of species population vs. time in years, starting with $N_0=100$:

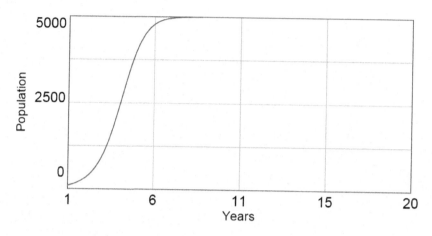

Figure III-13. Species Population vs Number of Years

The plot indicates that the population does indeed reach a steady-state after 6-7 years. By experimenting with this model (specifically the values of N_0) she also determines that both the steady-state population of 5,000 and the time required to get there are *very insensitive* to the initial seed population. Now she knows that she may proceed with the reintroduction using a small seed population of only ~100 individuals and expect to see a significant population increase within about 5 years.

By the way, you very rarely need to start from scratch when dynamic modelling. Many basic models have already been developed and published, and are widely available as starting points, which you may then adapt to your specific conditions. Here are a few of the basic models on isee's website: Housing Supply and Demand, Business Cycle Dynamics, Supply Chain Management, Predator-Prey Dynamics. And here are some in Barry Richmond's book (Richmond, 2004): Human

Resources Infrastructure, Customer Relationship, Administrative Main Chain Infrastructure, Manufacturing Main Chain, Sequential Work Flow Main Chain, Queue/Server Main Chain, Resource Allocation Infrastructure, Physical Capital Infrastructure, Financial Resources Infrastructure, and Political Capital Infrastructure.

In systems thinking, archetypes are ***problem-causing*** structures that are repeated in many situations, environments, and organizations. Being facile at identifying them is the first step in changing the destructive structure. There are 10 common archetypes (Bellinger, 2004a; Lawson, 2010; Meadows, 2008; Senge, 2006; Maani and Cavana, 2007):

1. Accidental adversaries
2. Fixes that fail (policy resistance)
3. Limits to growth
4. Shifting the Burden (addiction)
5. The tragedy of the commons
6. Drift to low performance (eroding goals)
7. Escalation
8. The rich get richer
9. Rule beating
10. Seeking the wrong goal

Each one is explained below.

1. **Accidental adversaries.** In accidental adversaries, 2 individuals or entities start collaborating, to their mutual benefit. It starts well, but then one does something that is perceived by the other to be damaging; so that individual reacts. Then the first person reacts to this, etc., in a death spiral. Examples include Sales versus Manufacturing, team members competing for a promotion, and employee versus the company. The problem is that we tend to interpret the actions of our teammate or partner as *adversarial*, when in fact the partner is guilty only

of pursuing a self-interest and neglecting the impact this would have on you. Local (versus systemic) thinking, mistrust, and poor communication contribute to this archetype. The solution: talk to your adversary and try to understand their logic. Explain your perception. Do not assume that he/she is out to get you.

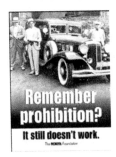

2. **Fixes that fail (policy resistance).** Some organizational or social systems have extremely strong stabilizing or balancing feedback loops. As a result, changes are counteracted by the feedback mechanism. So they are very hard to implement. Examples include the war on drugs, Prohibition of alcohol in the 1920s, elimination of our dependence on petroleum, and negative political campaigning. Some of these failed "fixes" were legislated. The solution: first, identify the reinforcing feedback loops and break them by installing incentives and rewards that will change behavior. Additionally, align individual goals with organizational goals. Finally, do not legislate morality; a free-market approach may yield better results (as it did with Prohibition).

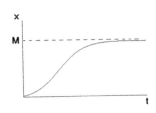

3. **Limits to growth**. All growth has some limit, be it due to market saturation, resource availability, overcrowding, competence limits, or inflexibility. Examples include rapid corporate growth followed by stagnation, reforms in education or healthcare followed by resistance, or the growth of bacteria. The solution: anticipate the limits and plan for

them; understand the balancing feedback loops that limit growth; develop new products, markets, and services; retrain and reeducate; understand life cycles and plan for them; and identify the strongest growth limiting factors.

 **4. Shifting the Burden (addiction).** In this archetype, an individual or organization depends upon someone or something else (the intervener) for success, happiness, etc. Examples include drug or alcohol addiction, a parent who regularly helps a child with her homework instead of letting her learn for herself, a government paying subsidies for farm products (butter or cheese) that would be unprofitable to sell in a free market, and government bailouts because banks are "too big to fail." Such intervention does not solve the root problem and disrupts the system's self-regulating feedback loops; it discourages personal, economic, and societal growth; and it also subverts the original purpose of the system. The solution: tough love; stop acting as a facilitator. It's OK to help with homework once in a while, but helping repeatedly develops a dependence and the child will not learn to figure things out on her own. Bailing out banks that made risky investments rewards them for making bad business decisions.

There are cases when shifting the burden (addiction) is good. I use a dentist to maintain my teeth, a doctor to maintain my health, and a tree service to prune my trees. Those are certainly examples of shifting the burden. I could get degrees in dentistry and medicine, take the risks associated with tree pruning, and do those tasks myself, but that would subvert my goals in life; it makes more sense for me to pay others to do those things for me. Addiction is bad when it subverts the optimal functioning of the system.

5. **The tragedy of the commons**. In this archetype, a shared resource (grass, land, water, air, fish, bison, IT services) is free or near-free and is therefore overused to the point of exhaustion. Since the resource is free there is competition to use as much of it as possible, resulting in rapid depletion. The depletion of finned fish off the coast of New England is a good example. Another good example is the overuse of IT services in a company because they are free, resulting in long backlogs. Solutions: coalitions and social agreements to limit consumption or laws that mandate this, or increasing the price of the resource through taxation or license fees. But before this can occur, a systems thinking analysis must be done to understand the cycle.

Figure III-14. The Extinct Passenger Pigeon

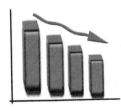

6. **Drift to low performance (eroding goals).** It's hard to maintain standards. In this archetype, an established standard is not met, so we settle for something that's not quite there, and this new lower goal becomes the new standard. Examples include the U. S. federal budget deficit, reduced exercise goals, and the acceptance of poorer scholastic performance by high school students. We drift a little from our original goals and see that nothing terrible happens, so the poorer performance becomes

the norm. This is short-term thinking! An excellent example is the U. S. President Obama's administration cutting standards for "No Child Left Behind" in 2011: "The Obama administration has been signaling since February of last year that it was getting ready to abandon a core component of the No Child Left Behind education reform law - 100 percent proficiency for all students in math and reading by 2014. And this month it did, announcing the availability of state waivers from the federal law's tough accountability measure." (Boston Globe, 8/22/2011). The solution: do not accept drift; hold goals absolute. When standards aren't met, change the system, not the standards.

7. **Escalation.** Escalation occurs when 2 entities become locked in vicious circle of ever-increasing threats, actions, or rhetoric, each trying to outdo the other. Examples include negative political campaigning, the US-USSR arms race in the 1960s, and gang violence. The solution: first understand, and then break the reinforcing feedback loop by backing out unilaterally or negotiating a truce.

8. **The rich get richer.** The world is a competitive place. In one manifestation of this archetype, successful competitors are rewarded with more means ($$, land, power, equipment) to be successful, so their wealth escalates. Unsuccessful competitors do not acquire more means and are

eventually eliminated from the market. In this way good business decision-makers are rewarded and provided more resources to make additional business decisions, and vice-versa. Examples are Steve Jobs and Apple and Bill Gates and Microsoft. But in a negative manifestation of "The rich get richer" wealthy people buy votes and promulgate laws that reduce their taxes while increasing taxes on the poor and middle classes. In another negative manifestation, poor children can't afford to go to college, remaining poor. The solutions: First of all, America is one of the few countries in the world where anyone can start a business at very low cost. People who were impoverished in their homeland can come to the U. S. and become successful. This is the result of reduced or eliminated barriers to entrepreneurship. Free or near-free education would help, as would a progressive taxation structure. "One man, one vote" democratizes the society and must be maintained instead of "one dollar, one vote."

9. **Rule beating**. In this archetype, people intentionally evade rules, policies, or guidelines, typically because they are perceived as unreasonable, unfair, too harsh, or unrepresentative of the people's will. Examples include alcohol prohibition in the 1920s in the U. S., marijuana laws, the 55 mph speed limit, and a no-talking policy. The solutions: a) ensure that those impacted by the rule are democratically involved in the rule-making b) clarify the intent of the rule and demonstrate the benefit to all, if there is one; if there isn't, eliminate or revise the rule. Great management doesn't derive from following the letter of the

law; it comes from understanding the intent of the rule and knowing when and how far you should bend the rules.

10. **Seeking the wrong goal.** A) The VP of Sales instituted a new bonus program for his sales staff: 10% of all sales above a cumulative $1 million threshold. Instantly, sales shot through the roof. And profits disappeared entirely. B) The VP of R & D offered a new incentive program to his staff: promotions based on the number of new products developed. New products proliferated rapidly. And not one was marketable. C) Standardized testing is intended to improve the quality of education. But it really just improves the quality of test-taking ability. These are examples of mis-stated or incorrect goals. The solution: ensure that the stated goal represents the desired end result and is an *end*, not a *means*. If the goal is to increase profits, do not articulate it as an increase in sales. If the goals is to develop new products that generate substantial profits, then state that.

These archetypes are common in organizations, societies, and relationships. Become familiar with them and learn to recognize them. Then, use the suggestions here to overcome them.

 Root cause analysis is a problem solving method aimed at determining the fundamental, or "root" cause of a problem. It involves tools such as "The Five Whys," fishbone diagrams, cause-and-effect diagrams, process flowcharts, runs charts, statistical process control charts, and Pareto diagrams. But conventional root-cause analysis often ends too early, ending with root causes such as "operator error," "mechanical failure," "design fault," or "insufficient training" (Galley, 2014). Although these are valid, they do not address the *underlying system or systems* that gave rise to those causes.

The 2011 Penn State football coach (Jerry Sandusky) child abuse situation is an example. Sandusky was an assistant coach for Penn State University, which boasted an excellent football team that had won the vast majority of the games it had played under head coach Joe Paterno. Sandusky used his position at the university, together with his charity organization *The Second Mile* to lure young football players into the system, where he sexually abused them. Several Penn State officials were aware of the abuse, but either ignored it or actively covered it up to protect the football program. Sandusky was tried and convicted, and the National Collegiate Athletic Association (NCAA) eventually imposed extraordinary penalties against the school, including vacating all football victories from 1998-2011 (Ganim, 2011). One might say that the issue was caused by a single perverse individual and a few administrators who looked the other way, but it was more than that: it was a *culture* (structure) that elevated football above all other societal values including

35

decency, integrity, and protecting our children. This was made clear by the NCAA sanctions which targeted a *fundamental change in the athletic culture and mentality* at Penn State.

Another example is the 1986 U. S. space shuttle Challenger disaster in which 7 astronauts lost their lives when a critical solid-fuel rocket O-ring failed shortly after take-off. Engineers knew about the O-ring issue; indeed failures or partial failures had been observed on previous launches, but none had been catastrophic. Because of this, NASA's culture changed from one of investigating each partial failure and correcting the issue to one of *accepting partial O-ring failures as the standard,* or expectation during shuttle missions.

Many systemic root-cause analyses lead to the system's underlying *culture* or *environment* as the systemic root cause. Other examples:

- The New Orleans, Louisiana (USA) hurricane Katrina disaster in 2005, in which more than 1000 people died, most by drowning due to floodwall and levee failures. Lake Pontchartrain sits at an elevation ~12 feet above New Orleans, just north of the city. Its waters are retained by a system of floodgates and levees, which were designed and maintained by the U. S. Army Corps of Engineers (USACE.) Water from several canals protruding into the city are also retained by a series of levees and floodwalls, also designed and maintained by the USACE. Analysis after the hurricane indicated the following root causes: the levee design was inadequate: they were too short and pilings were driven only half as deep as necessary, to save money. In addition, levee inspections were found to be largely ceremonial (Robertson, Campbell and Schwartz, 2015). Design calculation errors were made and there was inadequate external review. And political wrangling led to questionable compromises. A systemic perspective reveals that the levees were constructed piecemeal and never integrated into a complete hurricane protection *system*. But one of the greatest mistakes was a failure to properly quantify the risk of such a catastrophic storm. According to the American Society of Civil Engineers, "The levees and floodwalls breached because of a combination of unfortunate choices and decisions, made over many years, at almost all levels of responsibility." But what was the root-cause *system* that allowed all these engineering and policy failures to occur? It was a *culture of complacency* within both the USACE and politicians.

- The demise of Research In Motion (Canadian maker of Blackberry smart phones) after 2010 due to a culture of complacency and technological arrogance. This case is detailed later in Section V.

- The demise of U. S. energy corporation Enron in 2001 due to a corporate culture of greed, lying, and cheating. Enron grew to a $100 billion corporation under the brilliant and innovative marketing and business practices of its executives Kenneth Lay, Jeffrey Skilling, and Andrew Fastow. Unfortunately, they were a little too creative and fraudulently reported non-existent assets and earnings. When the fraud was discovered, the stock price plunged from >$100 per share to just pennies within a few months. The company filed for bankruptcy in late 2001, decimating thousands of employees' pension and 401k funds. Astoundingly, Enron's demise also brought down Arthur Andersen, one of the world's most prestigious accounting firms, due to obstruction of justice charges. Andersen was Enron's auditing company and was found to have intentionally destroyed documents pertinent to Enron's fraud investigation. The root cause in this case was a corporate culture of greed, lying, and cheating coupled with arrogance and creativity; all driven by the company's brilliant but unethical executives. One might go further and say that the root cause system was the American free enterprise, accounting, and business regulatory systems which permit (and even encourage) such transgressions.

- The British Petroleum *Deepwater Horizon* Gulf of Mexico oil rig explosion and oil spill of 2010 is the largest accidental marine oil spill in the history of the petroleum industry. Eleven people were never found and 4.9 million barrels of oil were discharged. Over 68,000 square miles (180,000 km^2) of ocean were impacted directly by the spill. Oil and sludge continued to be found on the shores of Louisiana, Tampa Bay, and the Florida (USA) panhandle, and dolphins and other marine life continued to die in record numbers through 2013. The cause of the explosion was a decision (based on a faulty pressure reading) by management to replace drilling fluid in the well with seawater, which was not dense enough to prevent the intrusion of methane gas into the well. The gas rose up the well pipe to the oil rig where it ignited, causing the explosion. The cause of the subsequent oil spill was found to be the failure of a cement barrier allowing hydrocarbons to flow up the wellbore and onto the oil rig, resulting in a blowout. The National Commission on the BP Deepwater Horizon Oil Spill and Offshore Drilling reported that BP did not use a diagnostic tool to test the strength of the cement and had ignored a pressure test that had failed. The Commission also reported that there had been "a rush to completion" on the well, criticized BP for poor management decisions, and stated that there was not a *culture of safety* on the oil rig. (National Commission, 2011). A report issued by the US government stated that the loss of life and pollution of the Gulf of Mexico were the result of poor risk management, last-minute changes to plans, failure to observe and respond to critical indicators, inadequate well control response, and insufficient emergency bridge response training by companies and individuals responsible for both drilling at the well and for the operation of the drilling platform (BOEMRE, 2011). The root cause of this disaster was a corporate culture of cost-cutting and not taking risks or safety seriously. As reported by the National Commission, "The immediate causes of the Macondo well blowout can be traced to a series of identifiable mistakes made by BP, Halliburton, and Transocean that reveal such systematic failures in risk management that they place in doubt the safety culture of the entire industry."

- The collapse of the Boston Red Sox baseball team in September of 2011. The Red Sox were well positioned to win the American League East and reach the World Series at the beginning of the 2011 season. However, the Red Sox lost 18 of their final 24 games, and finished in third place in their division with a record of

90 wins and 72 losses. On the last day of the season, the Red Sox lost to the Baltimore Orioles and were eliminated from postseason competition. Shortly after the season ended, several elite Red Sox pitchers admitted to playing video games, eating fried chicken, and drinking beer in the clubhouse. When not pitching games, they were absent from the dugout to support their teammates. They also cut back on their exercise regimens despite repeated appeals from the team's conditioning coach Dave Page. Team manager Terry Francona seemed more interested in being the players' friend than their coach, and lost his ability to address such lax behavior (Hohler, 2011). The entire debacle could be characterized by a management culture of laissez-faire and friendship in the clubhouse, instead of discipline and coaching.

- The culture of the Boston Red Sox baseball team stands in stark contrast to that of the New England Patriots football team. Under the guidance of owner Robert Kraft and head coach Bill Belichik, the Patriots have won more Super Bowls by a coach-quarterback team, appeared in more Super Bowls, and completed more Super Bowl touchdown passes than any other team in National Football League history. Yet they do not spend huge sums of money on their elite players. Instead, they maintain a culture of discipline, ego suppression, sacrifice of all interests for the benefit of the team, and hard work. They view the team as a complex system in which the mental models and relationships among the players are vital to team success. The prospect of a player ignoring the coach's directive is laughable. Interviews with players are noteworthy because of their failure to ever mention a word about themselves as individuals. This culture is perhaps best described by the mantra, "Do your job." The Patriots have established a legacy of success by virtue of their corporate culture of selflessness, teamwork, systems thinking, and discipline.

When conventional root cause analysis leads to a conclusion such as "user error," "operator error," "design flaw," or "insufficient training," do not accept that as the ultimate root cause. Instead, ask "what was the *environment* or *culture* that led to user error or insufficient training?" Is it one of laissez-faire in which user competence is not evaluated? Is it one in which competence and/or knowledge of procedures is *assumed*? Is it one of intimidation, such that people who do not know the correct procedures are afraid to ask for help? Or is it one where the values of the executives are inconsistent with the corporate mission? Users, operators, and designers make mistakes for reasons: figuring out those underlying reasons is systemic root cause analysis. As mentioned before, often the systemic root cause is the system's culture or environment.

So, what if you determine that the culture needs to change? Changing corporate culture is hard—how can you change values? The existing corporate culture exists for a reason—it serves the needs of a lot of people, and there are many reinforcing feedback loops. But Lou Gerstner changed the culture at IBM, and Alan Mullaly did it at Ford.

To change corporate culture:

- You must have an honest, real, and plausible, convincing argument regarding why the new culture will be better (e.g. a losing season, financial losses, high turnover, poor morale) and you must articulate it.

- The guy at the top must really want to change it.
- The VPs, directors, and managers must really want to, but you may have to get rid of some.
- You must convince all employees that changing the culture will benefit them personally.
- Involve your employees as change leaders so they are vested, and reward them for leading change.
- You must re-do your Goals/Rewards personnel incentive system to reward desired behaviors and punish undesired behaviors.
- You must change the structures that reinforced the old paradigm.
- You must be willing to get rid of non-performers and hire in new people who espouse the new culture.

But it's still hard.

There are several additional systems thinking tools that may be useful in certain circumstances:

Systemigrams. Systemigrams are diagrams depicting a system's concepts, actors, events, patterns, and processes in a single-page storyboard format, using color-coding to indicate similar or linked ideas. Although they include elements of causal loop diagrams, the main purpose of systemigrams is to tell a story describing the system. Details of systemigrams may be found in both Sauser (2015) and Boardman and Sauser (2008).

Interpretive Structural Modeling (ISM). ISM is a computer-aided process that transforms vague, poorly-defined concepts into clear graphic representations of systemic structures. This technique identifies those elements that most strongly influence, and those that are most strongly influenced by other systemic elements. ISM is explained in detail by Warfield (1974), Attri *et al.* (2013), and Lendaris (1980).

IV. Self-Organization and Emergence

Figure IV-1. Bird Murmuration, an emergent systemic property

A spectacular characteristic of systems is their exhibition of emergent properties: systemic properties that cannot be predicted from the characteristics of the system components, but that derive from the *relationships* among the components or between the components and the environment. Examples include the flocking of birds, V formations of geese, schooling of fish, ant colony structure, termite "cathedrals", pressure of gases, and entropy or disorder. Examples of emergence in human-designed systems include the meaning of words, traffic jam patterns, reliability, security, usability, countries, and the power of religion to influence behavior. Emergent properties often dominate systemic behavior, and since emergence cannot be predicted from the system components, linear, dissective, reductionist analysis cannot be used to understand emergent properties.

Emergence often derives from self-organization. Camazine says: "Self-Organization is a process in which a pattern at the global level of a system emerges solely from numerous interactions among the lower level components of the system. Moreover, the rules specifying interactions among the system's components are executed using only local information, without reference to the global pattern. In other words, the pattern is an emergent property of the system, rather than a property imposed on the system by an external influence." (Camazine et al, 2001)

Self-organization is present whenever a pattern develops as a result of the interactions of system components. No central plan or central planner need exist for systems to self-organize. Geese self-organize into V-formations. Molecules self-organize into elaborate crystals. Fish self-organize into schools and birds into flocks. Humans self-organize into groups or teams. This self-organization derives from either *mental models* in human-designed systems or from very basic laws or rules such as electrochemical attraction, minimization of chemical potential, hydrophilicity, minimization of surface energy, hydrodynamic forces, or entropy in natural systems.

Since emergent properties often dominate system behavior, it is important to be aware of them and to try to anticipate them. This is hard, but not impossible, by using morphological analogies or past history: groups of autonomous entities will likely exhibit coordinated movements (as do birds, fish, cars, and flotillas). Complex networks will more likely exhibit self-organization and possibly self-awareness. System components that display attractive and repulsive regions will organize themselves in a way that minimizes total energy.

V. Examples of Good and Bad Systems Thinking

The following examples demonstrate how systems thinking, or lack thereof, can have a significant impact on innovation in dynamically changing business environments, and business growth in existing and new markets.

Research in Motion versus Apple

:::BlackBerry One example is the Blackberry smart phone (Gustin, 2013). In 1999, the Canadian company Research In Motion (RIM) launched the Blackberry which provided secure access to corporate e-mail systems. By 2007, RIM had the lion's share of the smartphone market, based largely on the Blackberry's embedded QWERTY keyboard, top-notch security, and other innovative features, such as the Blackberry Messenger (BBM) service and Blackberry Curve. At that time, the company had over 10 million subscribers and was worth over 67 Billion. Blackberry was the device of choice by the government, many universities, and most businesses requiring high security and inexpensive messaging. However, the company grew complacent as competitors like Apple and Samsung began to out-innovate them. Apple had been entrenched in the consumer market and RIM in the business market, but in 2007 Apple decided to move into the business market, RIM's stronghold, with the introduction of the iPhone.

Apple approached this using Systems Thinking to drive innovation, creating new ways in which customers could use smartphones: specifically, new features and applications such as an intuitive user interface, touchscreen navigation, the App store, and iTunes store. Clearly, Apple saw the smartphone as more than just a communications device. They invented new ways that a small, portable, electronic device with local intelligence could be used to make people's lives more convenient and more fun. Samsung quickly followed suit. But RIM rested on its market share laurels and did little to bring new features to its customers. With limited vision, they were slow to realize that smartphones were evolving to become mobile entertainment devices. The interesting thing is that any smartphone user could have described the features and services that RIM needed to add to the Blackberry to remain competitive, but RIM management were asleep at the helm. When RIM finally launched a touchscreen device, it was viewed as an inadequate imitation of the iPhone. In January 2012, both co-CEOs stepped down and were replaced by Thorsten Heins, who had joined the company in 2007. In September 2013, the company announced a loss of almost $1 billion due to unsold inventory. To date, Heins has been unsuccessful in turning the company around.

This is an unfortunate example of non-innovative, linear thinking. Blackberry continued to view its products as mobile e-mail devices for corporate users, while Apple and Samsung envisioned smartphones evolving to become mobile entertainment devices for consumers, while also providing e-mail services with a more user-friendly interface. Clearly, Blackberry could have benefited from Systems Thinking by gaining an understanding of the bigger picture and emerging new market opportunities in advance of its competitors.

 On the other hand, Systems Thinking has facilitated innovation for some excellent companies like Apple Computer. In the 1980s and 1990s, personal music players had already made an appearance. The music players of this era were large, clunky, ungainly devices as shown in Figure V-1:

Figure V-1. Personal Music Players of the 1980s and 90s

There were basically 4 kinds with varying degrees of portability and capacity, as shown on the following "Dimensions of Design" plot:

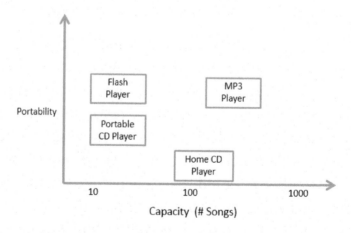

Figure V-2. Capacity versus Portability

When Apple entered the market in 2001, they could have simply extended the capacity and portability of existing devices, as shown below:

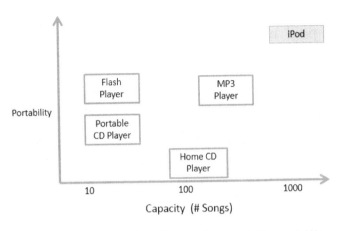

Figure V-3. iPod's Capacity and Portability

However, this simple extension of existing technologies would have been linear thinking. Instead, they used Systems Thinking by considering a completely new dimension of design: sexiness, coolness, prestige, aesthetics—none of which had been previously considered in portable music player design. This may be considered a 3rd dimension on the design space plot:

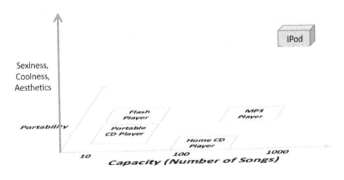

Figure V-4. The Jobsian 3rd Dimension

Would Apple have taken over the market without this cool 3rd dimension? Possibly—however it would likely have taken longer and been less effective. It is noteworthy that in the subsequent design evolution of the iPod, as much attention has been paid to the aesthetics and cool factor as to the functionality, as shown in Figure V-5:

Figure V-5. iPod Evolution

This is an excellent example of Systems Thinking applied to innovation in product design.

However, Apple went far beyond product design in using Systems Thinking to innovate. For the iPod to really catch on, a system had to be developed that facilitated the downloading of music from the Internet. This required not only the technology, but also consideration of ancillary factors such as licensing, royalties, payment and transaction management, and storage. By addressing each of these with the development of iTunes, Apple not only enabled the iPod, but it completely disrupted existing music listening technology (CDs).

Why Is This Systems Thinking? In *Designing for People*, Don Norman says, "It is *not* about the iPod; it is about the **system**. Apple was the first company to license music for downloading. It provides a simple, easy to understand pricing scheme. It has a first-class website that is not only easy to use but fun as well. The purchase, downloading the song to the computer and thence to the iPod are all handled well and effortlessly. And the iPod is indeed well designed, well thought out, a pleasure to look at, to touch and hold, and to use. There are other excellent music players. No one seems to understand the systems thinking that has made Apple so successful." (Norman, 2009).

The iPod is not a stand-alone product; instead it is part of a personal entertainment *system,* the elements of which include the iPod itself, the individual who is listening, the environment (indoors, outdoors, office, gym, etc.), the songs, the song acquisition and storage, and the activities while listening (whether jogging, studying, relaxing, spinning, driving, etc.). The iPod Personal Entertainment System is not a product at all; it is a *service*. It is experienced, not consumed. Apple's recognition of this and that the device itself is simply an element of this service was not only innovative, but revolutionary. While other manufacturers (Sony, Tascam, Microsoft, Diamond) structured their companies to support the *device* that they manufactured, Apple structured their company to support the *user*:

Figure V-6. Apple's User-Centric Systems Philosophy

The iPad was developed using similar innovative Systems Thinking. It is natural to ask if other products should be considered through this innovative Systems Thinking "experiencing" versus "owning" lens:

- The automobile versus the *car buying and owning experience*? Some dealerships have already started down this path with service areas that provide free meals, entertainment, and drop-off services.

- Coffee versus the *coffee-drinking experience*? Starbucks (and others) attracts clients to not only buy and drink coffee, but to enjoy the coffeehouse experience, with free wi-fi, comfortable seating, and even fireplaces in some establishments.

- Clothes versus the clothes *buying and owning experience*?

- Flat Panel TV versus the *home entertainment system experience*?

Polaroid versus Samsung

◆Polaroid Another example (Nagy Smith, 2009) is the U. S. photography/ film company Polaroid, once considered a stellar example of a high-tech success that rose to market dominance in instant photography as a result of the innovative products developed by its founder, Edwin Land. Instant photography was based on innovations in chemistry and film, or photographic chemistry, which Land considered to be his legacy. As electronic imaging technology began to mature, Polaroid was well aware of this trend and by 1989 was spending 42% of its research and development budget on digital imaging. By 1990, Polaroid was the number one provider of digital cameras.

Despite its early lead in the digital camera market, however, it failed to take full advantage of the emerging trends in digital photography such as purely digital work flow. Senior management continued to believe that customers wanted hard-copy print, rather than electronic images that could be viewed on digital displays and in slide shows. The company had a bias against electronics, even though it had made significant investments in its Micro-Electronics Laboratory in the mid-1980s, and the significant profitability of their film business (with gross margins of over 65%) made the consideration of new business models and markets out of the question. As digital cameras became commodities, resolution increased, and customers realized the speed and cost-savings associated with digital work flow, Polaroid began losing its largest customers in the real estate and photo-identification markets, and its sales of film dropped precipitously. As a result, Polaroid filed for bankruptcy in October 2001, and never recovered.

Unfortunately, this was an example of linear thinking. Although the company instructed its researchers to develop digital cameras in response to emerging trends in digital photography, the focus was on developing digital cameras that could produce hard-copy print, without a better understanding of the bigger picture and emerging new market opportunities. Polaroid's innovation was limited by its linear-thinking while competitors such as Canon, Nikon, and even Kodak (to a degree) were better systems thinkers.

 Korean electronics giant Samsung has also used Systems Thinking to innovate. In 2000, Samsung was not known for product quality. Its products were known for frequent breakdowns and mediocre quality. As recently as 2001, Samsung's only goal was to catch up with its Japanese rivals. Per Wikipedia, Samsung now is outperforming major Japanese electronics makers in many categories: in terms of global market share, Samsung is No. 1 in flat-panel TVs and memory chips; it is No. 2 in mobile handsets; it is one of the top suppliers in other home appliances. Between 2002 and 2013 Samsung's sales increased from $40 billion to $220 billion:

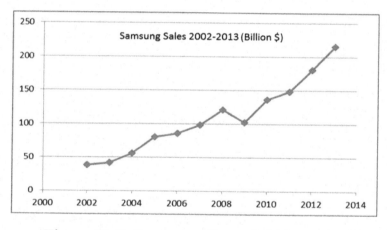

Figure V-7. Samsung Growth 2000-2013

How did Samsung achieve this meteoric rise in only 10 years? They could have used linear thinking: "Our product quality is poor, so let's improve it; our sales will grow as customers become aware of the improved quality." But that would have been a slow, tedious approach to gaining market share. Instead, Samsung used Systems Thinking: "We have had poor quality; simply improving product quality is necessary but will not generate new customers quickly. Therefore we must demonstrate to existing customers our interest in fixing quality and we must build trust and confidence." As a result, Samsung restructured their customer service function to deliver outstanding service, one element of which was to accept almost all warranty claims (trust the customer).

This philosophy is illustrated with a real-life example. In 2003, I owned a Samsung flat-panel monitor. One Saturday morning there was an electrical storm and our power went out. When the power came back on, the power surge blew out the monitor. I looked in the monitor's service manual for a customer support number and was surprised to find it on the first page, in big, bold, black font. Since it was Saturday, I figured I'd call the number and leave a message. I was shocked when a live human being answered the phone. After trying several trouble-shooting ideas, none of which worked, he asked me for my address. I asked, "Why do you need my address?" The customer service representative responded "To send you a replacement monitor." I asked if he wanted the monitor's serial number, date of purchase, etc., and he responded, "No. It's our product, it doesn't work, and you are entitled to have a functional device. When you receive the new monitor, please ship back the old one in the same packing material" and he gave me a Returned Material Authorization (RMA) number. That was Saturday. I received the replacement monitor the following Tuesday.

This is an interesting example of using Systems Thinking to innovate not the product itself, but the service and support structure around the product to build consumer trust and confidence.

VI. Cookbook Examples

Example #1. The Selling System at New England Digital Controls

A Systems Thinking Case Study

New England Digital Controls, Inc. is a $100 million company specializing in digital control hardware and software using proprietary technology. The company has offices in Burlington, MA, London, Paris, and Berlin and employs 300 people world-wide. It also uses a loose-knit web of manufacturers' representatives, both in the U.S and abroad. Its products include both stand-alone controllers and large, complicated turnkey control systems (involving housings, power sources, wiring, sensors, relays, switches, transformers, and panels) into which the controllers are placed. Principal markets include military (drones, tanks, ships, other vehicles, robots, weapons), automotive, the fluids handling industry (pumping and piping systems, tank level controls, flow controls, etc.), and consumer products (electronics, washers, dryers, dishwashers, ovens, music reproduction equipment, home theater, TVs, radios, etc.). Sales are ~evenly split among these 4 market segments. About 50% of gross sales derive from the Americas while 50% derive from Europe and Asia. The company comprises 5 major divisions: Sales, Operations (manufacturing), R & D, Accounting, and Applications Engineering.

The Americas Sales Organization has historically been problematic for this company. Over the past 10 years, sales have been flat while the industry has grown. In addition, there has been a revolving door of sales directors and the average tenure in the job has been ~2 years. There is a good deal of friction between the sales organization and the other principal functionalities (R & D, Operations, Accounting) within the company. For example, the sales director frequently asks R & D to develop new products that have only 1-off or very small market application; this creates a huge burden and backlog of development requests for R & D. The sales organization often promises customer deliveries that are impossible for Operations to achieve. Because Sales knows that Operations will probably deliver late, they often order much more product than the customer has ordered and store the excess remotely, and they often claim that they need the material well before it is actually needed by the customer. Sales generates a list of sales prospects each month. Operations has tried to use this list to build products that are likely to be sold in the near-term, but this has proven disastrous as the sales projections are badly off. And Accounting is suspicious that sales people often "pad" their expense reports, take long lunches, use their company car for personal business or pleasure, and attend sales meetings in exotic places. One month, a sales employee had $10,000 in business credit card debt but could only find receipts for ~$2,000. In another case, after a hard day's work, a sales engineer ordered a $100 glass of cognac after dinner. In a third case, it was discovered that a sales engineer was intentionally booking long, circuitous flights to garner frequent-flyer miles that he would subsequently use for personal vacations. Because of the mistrust that these and similar actions have created, sales has never been provided the actual factory cost of any of the company's products; they are provided only list prices. Any customer discounts off list must be approved by both the Sales Director and the company president. This has resulted in sales often disguising discounts as customer samples, trials, etc. Purchases of office equipment, supplies, computers, smart phones, travel items, gasoline, etc., must also be approved by all levels. Approvals sometimes take a long time. Sales have developed creative ways to circumvent this approval process, for example, by charging expenses on their personal credit cards and then burying those expenses in travel expense reports. In addition, because Accounting mistrusts sales, they scrutinize all sales expense reports in much greater detail than anyone else's. Sales realizes this and takes it as a personal challenge to pull one over on Accounting. The last Sales Director defended his staff rabidly, but this only increased the friction between him and the other division managers in R & D, Operations, and Accounting.

Structure: The Americas sales force is split into 5 geographic regions, each with a regional sales manager (RSM). Most RSMs have BS degrees in electrical engineering as well as capital equipment sales experience. Some RSMs live and work in the geographic regions that they serve; however 3 of the 5 live in Massachusetts, near NEDC headquarters. Some regions have 1 or more sales engineers reporting to the RSM while some have none. The business volume and profitability vary greatly among the 5 regions. The 5 RSMs collaborate with each other, but they also compete. Serious battles occur when RSMs must share sales credit; e.g. when the headquarters of a customer lie in 1 region but the operating division lies in another.

Accounting: There are accounting reports (monthly Profit and Loss; plan versus actual) for the Americas sales department as a whole. There are no accounting reports for the 5 individual sales regions. The RSMs calculate monthly regional sales themselves. The total from the 5 regions invariably differs from the accounting reports.

Support: Most systems sales require pilot testing, which involves tests at the customer's site using a large, heavily-instrumented pilot system along with an applications engineer to execute the tests. New England Digital Controls has an Applications Engineering Department along with a department head. All requests for pilot testing must go from the RSM to the Sales Director for approval, then to the Applications Engineering department head, who approves or rejects requests and then schedules the pilot tests (both the systems and the applications engineer) for approved requests. Pilot testing typically takes between 2 weeks and 2 months but there is usually a backlog of 3-4 months. The pilot test requestor is not charged directly for the pilot tests; instead all pilot test expenses are charged to the Americas Sales budget. RSMs and regional sales engineers complain loudly and often that delays in pilot testing limit sales. This just antagonizes the Applications Engineering Manager who is not motivated to be responsive to the sales organization, since they seem to complain about everything, no matter what. There are standardized test procedures for each of the 4 major market applications; however there is very little documentation on the test procedures and most of this knowledge resides in the heads of the Applications Engineers. The Applications Engineering turnover rate is 32% per year.

The digital control systems are warrantied. The warranty is typically provided by the sales organization. About 15% of the time, these warranties result in warranty claims that consume a good deal of money and time of the applications engineers, who are called upon to correct all warranty issues.

Accountability, Incentives: The sales people receive bonuses each year, based on sales volume. Warranty claims do not enter into bonus calculations. Individual bonus amounts are left to the discretion of the Americas Sales Director. A Sales Plan is developed in December of each year for the following calendar year. No one in the company (other than the sales director) knows which sales people hit their targets each year.

There are 3-5 manufacturers' representatives in each geographic region; these take direction from the RSMs but do not actually report to them as they carry several product lines in addition to NEDC's. The representatives serve mostly as "finders" and get a sales commission for every sale made:

Table VI-I. Representative Commission Structure

Value of Sale	Commission % of Sale
<$10,000	12%
$10,001-$100,000	8%
$100,001-$500,000	5%
>$500,000	2%

About 98% of representative-generated sales are for systems <$10,000.

You have just taken over as the V. P. of Americas Sales---Congratulations! It is your job to correct the deficiencies in this system and get sales and profit back on a growth track.

Apply the Systems Thinking Methodology:

Step 1. **Develop and articulate a problem statement**. The problem is "Declining sales and profit because of the relationships between Sales and the rest of the organization."

Step 2. **Identify and delimit the system**. Tools: Block Diagram, Organizational Chart, Causal Loop Diagrams (CLDs). For this problem, a block diagram and organizational chart are sufficient to delimit the system.

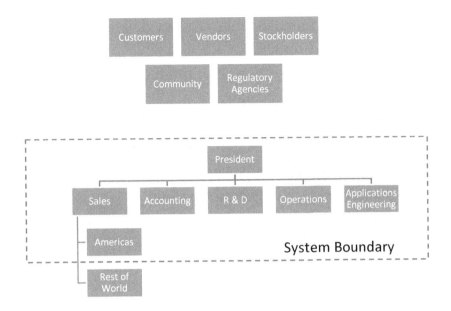

Figure VI-1. System Delimitation

Including customers, vendors, stockholders, the community, and regulatory agencies is probably too broad and unnecessarily complicates the analysis. On the other hand, limiting the system to just the Sales organization is too narrow. The dashed line shows a reasonable system boundary.

Step 3. **Identify the Events and Patterns**. Tools: Iceberg Model, Behavior-Over-Tome (BOT) Graphs. For this problem, simply listing the events and patterns (there are a lot!) should suffice, since they are already clearly articulated in the narrative:

- Repeated new Sales Directors
- Friction between Americas Sales and other departments
- Invalid product development requests from Sales

- Repeated unreasonable product delivery promises by Sales to customers
- Repeated over-ordering of product by Sales
- Frequent Sales giveaways
- Poor sales projections
- Unreasonable Sales expense reports
- Over-scrutiny of Sales expense reports
- Continuous pilot testing backlog
- Regular Sales complaints about pilot testing
- Warranty claims
- Annual sales plan of questionable value

Step 4. **Discover the Structures**. Tools: Iceberg Model, Causal Loop Diagrams, Stock-and-Flow diagrams, simple verbal description. Many of the existing structures are best described using simple verbiage; some benefit from causal loop diagrams. It's important to remember that the structures are caused by mental models and that the structures, in turn, yield events and behavior patterns.

Structure 1. The reporting relationships of the Regional Sales Managers and the Applications Engineers. These reporting relationships (each to separate supervisors) do not encourage teamwork or collaboration.

Structure 2. The Goals-Behaviors-Metrics-rewards (GBMR) System. As it is, this system rewards Sales for sales volume regardless of profit; it does not include warranty expenses as a Sales responsibility, it does not hold Sales accountable to any degree for missed deliveries, and it does not hold the non-Sales functions of the company accountable for contributing to sales success.

Structure 3. There are no regional accounting metrics nor are Regional Sales Managers held accountable for their regions' profitability.

Structure 4. All discounts off list price must be approved by both the Sales Director and the President; all Sales expenses (even trivial ones) must also be approved.

Structure 5. New Product Requests. The existing structure seems to give Sales free range to request whatever they want, regardless of market justification.

Structure 6. Pilot testing procedures. Requesting a pilot test is onerous and cumbersome; also Regional Sales Managers are not charged for them.

Structure 7. The expense report system.

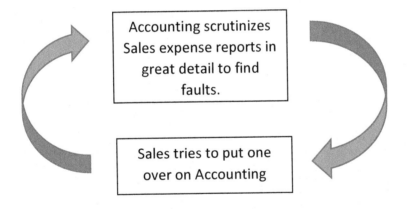

Figure VI-2. Expense Report Reinforcing Feedback Loop

Structure 8. Sales requests.

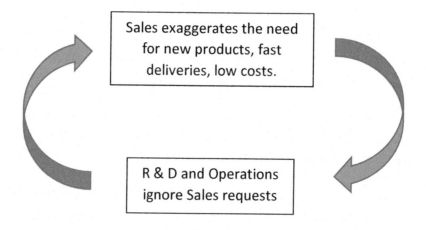

Figure VI-3. Sales Request Reinforcing Feedback Loop

Structure 9. Information availability.

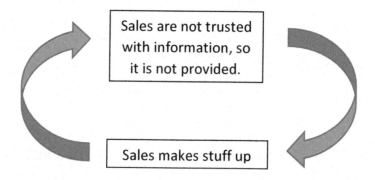

Figure VI-4. Information Reinforcing Feedback Loop

Step 5. **Discover the Mental Models**. Tools: Iceberg Model. First, let's just list the mental models:

Mental Models held by Americas Sales:

1. Accounting is out to get me.
2. Operations is always late on delivery.
3. R & D can't deliver the new products that I need.
4. No one likes or trusts Sales.
5. I can't do my job without critical data (such as costs) and support in the form of pilot tests, new products, and competitive deliveries. This company doesn't get it.

Mental Models held by the rest of the organization:

1. Bonuses will incentivize sales to sell more.
2. Manufacturers' Representatives should be limited with respect to how much they earn selling NEDC products.
3. Warranties are a necessary evil.
4. The Sales organization cannot be trusted. They cheat on their expense reports, they giveaway stuff that they shouldn't, they order more than they need, they commit to impossible deliveries, and they are used car salesmen.

Once identified, these mental models can be used in the Iceberg Model:

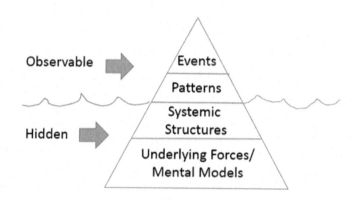

Figure VI-5. Iceberg Model

Specific Iceberg Models are presented here in tabular form in Tables VI-II and VI-III:

Table VI-II. Iceberg Models for American Sales

Mental Model	Resulting Structure	Pattern	Events
Accounting is out to get me.	Escalation – displayed between Sales and Accounting with respect to expense reports.	Sales continues to try to put one over on Accounting.	Unreasonable expense reports; Sales padding expense reports.
Operations is always late on delivery.	Escalation – displayed between Sales and Operations with respect to customer orders and delivery times.	Sales exaggerates the need for fast deliveries, larger order amounts and low costs.	Growing Operations backlog; excess inventory stored remotely; Operations ignores Sales requests.
R&D can't deliver the	Escalation – displayed	Sales exaggerates the	Growing R&D backlog of new

products that I need.	between Sales and R&D with respect to new products.	need for new products that are 1-off or have very small markets.	product development requests; R&D ignores Sales requests.
We don't trust Sales.	A structure of excessive scrutiny, rigid rules and procedures, and limits on information provided.	Lack of cooperation and teamwork between Sales and the other departments. Escalation.	Growing friction between Sales and the other departments.
I can't do my job without critical data (such as costs) and support in the form of pilot tests, new products, and competitive deliveries. This company doesn't get it.	Refusal by Sales to accept responsibility for sales figures; a structure of blaming other departments.	Sales makes stuff up and blames others.	Sales projections are way off; Operations builds too many products or the wrong products; Growing Operations and R&D backlogs.

Table VI-III. Iceberg Models for the Rest of the Organization

Mental Model	Resulting Structure	Pattern	Events
Sales compensation based on sales volume will incentivize Sales to sell more.	Sales people receive bonuses each year, based on sales volume, not profitability. Warranty claims do not enter into bonus calculations.	Declining sales and profit.	Discounted product sales and sales giveaways; significant number of costly warranty claims.

Manufacturers' Representatives should be limited with respect to how much they earn selling NEDC products.	Regressive commission structure for Manufacturers' Representatives.	Manufacturers' Representatives focus on sales of low-cost products.	Large volume of sales of lower cost products with lower profits.
Warranties are a necessary evil. Sales should not be accountable for them.	Warranties are provided by Sales without regard to cost or bonuses.	Warranties result in warranty claims 15% of the time.	Warranty claims consume a good deal of money and time of the application engineers.
The Sales organization cannot be trusted.	Accidental Adversaries - displayed between Sales and the other departments.	Lack of cooperation and teamwork between Sales and the other departments.	Growing friction between Sales and the other departments. Low profit.

Step 6. Identify and Address Archetypes. Many of the 10 archetypes are manifested here. However, the following 4 are the most significant:

1. *Accidental Adversaries.* Displayed between Sales and the other departments; and also between the Regional Sales Managers in the Americas Sales organization.
2. *Tragedy of the Commons.* Displayed by the Americas Sales Organization RSMs as they compete with each other for pilot testing equipment and time.
3. *Escalation.* Displayed between Sales and Operations with respect to delivery times; between Sales and R & D with respect to new products; and between Sales and Accounting with respect to expenses.
4. *Rule-Beating.* Displayed by Americas Sales with respect to requests for new products, requests for pilot

testing, inappropriate expense reports, and disguising discounts.

Step 7. **Model (if appropriate)**. Tools: Stock-and-Flow Diagrams, System Dynamics software.

Step 7a. Develop the Model.

Step 7b. Validate the Model.

Step 7c. Identify Leverage Points.

Step 7d. Optimize.

Modeling does not seem to be necessary for this situation. Indeed, it would be difficult to model accurately the impact of trust or mistrust on company profitability.

Step 8. **Systemic Root Cause Analysis**. This one is easy. The fundamental systemic root cause is organizational mistrust, which is a cultural issue. To correct the problems with this company, mutual trust will need to be restored. See pages 41 - 42 for suggestions on changing corporate culture.

Step 9. **Make recommendations**. The fundamental problem is the mistrust between the Americas Sales organization and the other departments, along with the structures and archetypes that have resulted. To address this problem, trust must be restored, mental models must change, and destructive structures must be torn down and new ones established. Here are recommendations:

1. As the new Sales V.P. you must have unimpeachable ethics and the backbone to enforce them.
2. Develop a new vision for the Sales organization and how it meshes with the rest of the company. Include honesty, fairness, and integrity as core values.

3. Replace any Sales personnel who refuse to embrace those principles.
4. Re-structure the organization to have Applications Engineering report to the Sales Director. They are a selling resource.
5. Construct Sales teams consisting of a sales person and an Applications Engineer.
6. Revise employee review and compensation plans so that the Applications Engineers and the Sales Engineers are both incented and rewarded based on *net profitability* of the region that they serve. Include pilot test costs and warranty expenses in these calculations.
7. Eliminate most required approvals. Provide the Regional Sales Managers ample authority (within limits) to discount list prices and to make regional purchases required to run their regions. The correct incentive structure (see above) will provide ample feedback so that they make good business decisions.
8. New Sales V. P. meet with the other departments:
    a. Articulate the new vision.
    b. Accept responsibility for past transgressions.
    c. Commit to change.
    d. In exchange, demand support for the Sales organization, which pays everyone's salary:
        i. Competitive costs
        ii. Competitive deliveries
        iii. Competitive products
        iv. Fair treatment in all areas, but especially by Accounting with respect to expenses
9. Change the structure by which R & D decides which new products to develop. Base it upon market demand and potential profit.

10. Eliminate the onerous pilot test request/approval structure and replace it with one requiring no approvals but holding the Regional Sales Managers accountable for pilot test costs and their impact on net profit.
11. Change the representative commission structure from regressive to progressive to encourage more big sales.
12. Flood the Sales organization with information, including cost data, and demonstrate trust.
13. Install metrics to measure sales performance *by region*, especially net profitability. Include warranty costs. Charge each region for pilot test costs and, in fact, for all costs associated with the region.
14. Establish regular meetings (perhaps lunches) among the directors of Sales, R & D, Operations, and Accounting to address issues and progress.

Step 10. **Assess Improvement**. Once changes have been implemented, the system behavior must be reassessed to determine if there has been improvement. If it is insufficient, the procedure begins again with Step 1.

Example #2. Measles Vaccinations.

Measles is a serious disease that can have long-term complications such as pneumonia, encephalitis, and hearing loss. Excellent vaccines are available that are 95% effective; however a bogus report published in *The Lancet* medical journal in 1998 linked measles vaccinations to autism in children. Although that fallacious report has been debunked, some parents refuse to have their children vaccinated. Inoculation of a significant fraction of the populace is required to prevent epidemics. A common belief is that if everyone else has their kids vaccinated, then I don't need to.

Healthcare professionals need to understand the fears and anxieties (as well as the real health risks) caused by both the disease and the vaccine. Specifically, they need to know what percentage of the populace needs to be vaccinated and how much should be invested in a publicity campaign to achieve the required inoculation rate.

This problem is elucidated through the use of a dynamic model.

Apply the Systems Thinking Methodology:

Step 1. **Develop and articulate a problem statement.** The problem is that an insufficient number of parents are having their children inoculated against measles due to fear that the vaccination causes autism; the disease is spreading and some are becoming seriously ill while others are dying.

Step 2. **Identify and delimit the system.** The system includes the population of all children in the geography of concern as well as their parents, the healthcare systems, the news media, and the technical literature.

Step 3. **Identify the Events and Patterns.** More children are developing measles than in the past. A lower percentage of parents are having their children vaccinated. More serious measles side-effects (pneumonia, encephalitis, hearing loss) and some deaths are being observed. There is fear of autism associated with the measles vaccine.

Step 4. **Discover the Structures.** The structures are the healthcare system, the news reporting structure, the school and pre-school systems, and the insurance rules.

Step 5. **Discover the Mental Models**. Several mental models are at play here:

- Measles vaccines cause autism.
- I'd rather risk my child contracting measles than developing autism.
- If everyone else has their child vaccinated, then I do not need to vaccinate my child.
- People who do not vaccinate their children are putting my children at risk.
- People who do not vaccinate their children can create a serious epidemic.
- People who do not vaccinate their children are very foolish.

Step 6. **Identify and Address Archetypes**. Three archetypes are evident here: Accidental Adversaries, Tragedy of the Commons, and Drift to Low Performance. Those who want their children inoculated are adversaries of those who do not, believing the latter to be a threat to their families' health and well-being. By not requiring 100% inoculation (no child left unvaccinated) Drift to Low Performance is observed. And finally, if good health is viewed as a resource to which we are all entitled, Tragedy of the Commons manifests itself. Those who do not have their children vaccinated freeload off those who do.

Step 7. **Model (if appropriate).** This case lends itself especially well to dynamic modeling. Isee Systems Inc. of Lebanon, NH developed an excellent dynamic model for the spread of *influenza*, based on an SEIR (Susceptible, Exposed, Infected, Recovered) compartmental model developed by epidemiologists. We have adapted isee's model for measles using their Stella software.

First, here is the Stock-and-Flow Diagram:

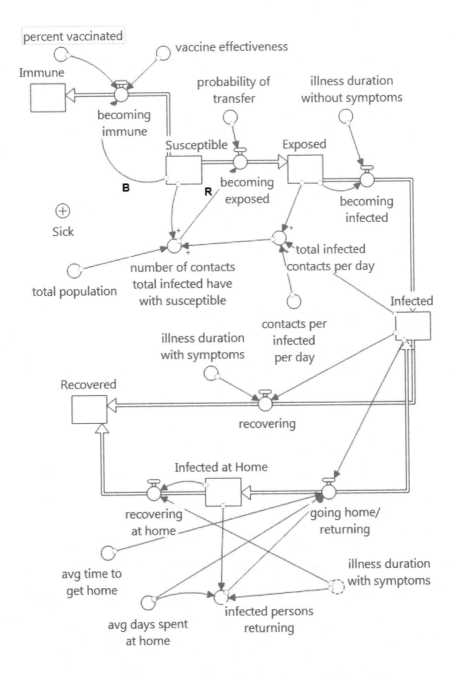

Figure VI-6. Measles Outbreak Stock-and-Flow Diagram,
adapted from isee Systems, Inc.

The equations for this dynamic model are available from the authors. The results are shown below:

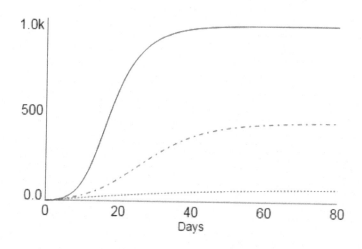

Figure VI-7. Measles Model Results

This plot shows the number of students infected with measles (out of a population of 1,000) following the introduction of the disease by 1 infected student at day 1. Three lines are shown: the blue line shows the infection rate over time with no students vaccinated; the red line with 50% of the students vaccinated, and the pink line with 80% vaccinated. With 50% vaccinated, the infection rate is ~40%; with 80% vaccinated, the infection rate is ~5%. This interesting result makes it clear that a 100% inoculation rate is *not necessary* to have good control over the spread of the disease.

Step 8. **Determine the systemic root cause(s).** A Fishbone Diagram is useful for elucidating the potential root causes of this situation:

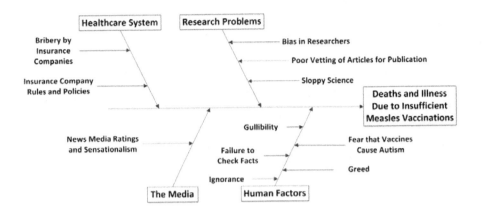

Figure VI-8. Measles Fishbone Diagram

Although root causes include the publication of bogus research results and a fear that the vaccinations will cause autism, the *systemic* root cause is a system that sensationalizes negative rare events, permits sloppy science and publication, and abdicates understanding of health risks to insurance companies.

Step 9. **Make recommendations.** With the data from the dynamic model, one can determine the cost in lives of various inoculation rates:

Table VI-IV. Deaths as a Function of Vaccination Rates

	Un-Vaccinated	50% Vaccinated	80% Vaccinated
Number Infected	500,000	200,000	25,000
Number of Deaths @ 0.3% Mortality	1,500	600	75

This table is based on a geography with a population of 5 million, 10% of whom are exposed to measles during an outbreak. It indicates that 525 lives are saved if the inoculation rate is increased from 50% to 80%. If human lives are valued at $6 million (a figure commonly used by insurance companies) then this represents a societal savings of over $3 billion. Whether you approve or disapprove of the monetary valuation of human life, 525 lives saved is a very significant number. The above table does not include the costs of healthcare for the thousands of unvaccinated individuals who do not die but who require expensive healthcare. It is clearly worthwhile to convince as many as possible to have their children vaccinated. To do this, their fear must be overcome.

The fear that measles vaccinations cause autism is based on an article that was published by Andrew Wakefield in the medical journal *The Lancet* in 1998. Subsequent investigators could not reproduce the data used as the basis for the article. Investigation revealed that Wakefield had been paid $675,000 by British lawyers who wanted to prove that the vaccine was dangerous, and that he was also attempting to market a competitive vaccine that he had developed. The link between autism and the vaccine was fully debunked in subsequent investigations, *The Lancet* published a retraction, and Wakefield was stripped of his medical license. Unfortunately, the news media publicized Wakefield's bogus claims, and several parents of children who had both been immunized and had developed problems unrelated to the immunization saw this as an opportunity to sue drug companies. No suits were successful.

To overcome the fear caused by *The Lancet* article, a publicity/information campaign exposing the truth must be waged. The costs of not vaccinating and the benefits of vaccinating must be clearly articulated and publicized. Public figures must be involved. Inasmuch as the cost of not vaccinating is in the billions, substantial resources must be made available for this campaign.

Step 10. **Assess Improvement.** Once changes have been implemented, the system behavior must be reassessed to determine if there has been improvement. If it is insufficient, the procedure begins again with Step 1.

Example #3. Using Systems Thinking to Deal With ISIS.

This example is condensed from Monat and Gannon (2015b); used with permission.

The Islamic State of Iraq and Syria (ISIS) is a jihadist organization of Sunni Muslims whose goal is world domination leading to the end of days, at which time the faithful will ascend to paradise. That path to paradise is via Jihad (Holy War), which ISIS must wage at least once per year. The atrocious acts of ISIS, such as beheadings, immolations, enslavement, and rape of infidel women, are designed to serve this goal by terrorizing its enemies leading to either capitulation or outright war. Another ISIS goal is to provide free housing, food, clothing, and health care to the people it rules. To achieve these goals, ISIS needs a Caliph, a territory that it controls, and continual expansion of that territory. ISIS also needs money and other resources to provide food, clothing, healthcare, weapons, and ammunition to its continually growing populace.

People join ISIS for a variety of reasons. Pious Sunni Muslims find ISIS appealing because of the promise of paradise to the faithful. The unemployed and disenfranchised find ISIS appealing because they can have a place to stay warm, have regular meals, get medical attention, and envision a path out of poverty and oppression. Those who seek power, control, and adventure find ISIS appealing because it offers them those opportunities (Hamid, 2015; McCants, 2015; Thompson, 2015; Von Drehle, 2015; Wood, 2015).

The behavior of ISIS appears to be self-destructive and illogical since their actions have united much of the world, including their Middle Eastern neighbors, against them. The following applies our methodology to analyze ISIS, which also illustrates how it can be used for other (non-ISIS) terrorist groups.

Apply the Systems Thinking Methodology:

Step 1. **Develop and articulate a problem statement**. The problem is that ISIS aspires to world domination and is intent upon killing, torturing, or enslaving all who do not adhere to its beliefs and principles.

Step 2. **Identify and delimit the system.** Tools: Block Diagram, Organizational Chart, Causal Loop diagrams, Verbal description. Inasmuch as ISIS aspires to dominate the entire world, all countries are part of the system of interest. However, it is useful to identify specific sub-groups within this system:

> *Religious Split:* ISIS supporters; Sunni Muslims who do not support ISIS, Shia Muslims, other Muslims, non-Muslims.

> *Geographic Split:* Iraq and Syria, neighboring countries, non-neighboring countries, the United States.

> *ISIS Demographic Split*: ISIS fighters, ISIS civilians; ISIS leaders.

Step 3. **Identify the Events and Patterns**. Tools: Causal Loop Diagrams (which also aid in the identification of structures).

Causal Loop 1: The U. S. as World Policeman: A Reinforcing Feedback Loop: In the current case, continued intervention by the U. S. in local conflicts reinforces the resentment of other countries toward the U. S., which (in turn) yields increased anti-American activity, which results in more American intervention.

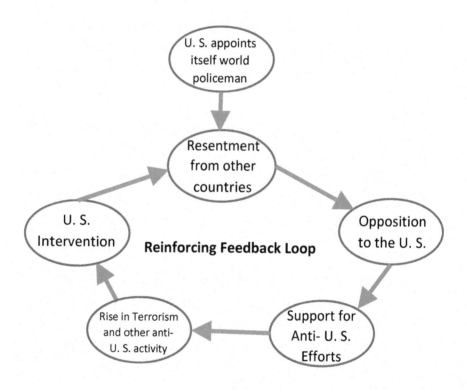

Figure VI-9. The U.S. as World Policeman.

Causal Loop 2: The Recurring Cycle of Arab Oppression:
Another example of a relevant reinforcing feedback loop is
the recurring cycle of oppression among competing political
regimes. As one regime is overthrown, another oppressive
regime emerges, and the vicious cycle continues.

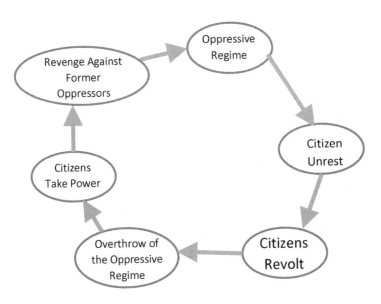

Figure VI-10. The Recurring Cycle of Arab Oppression.

Causal Loop 3: How the U. S. Contributed to the Rise of ISIS and Could Repeat this Mistake: As shown in the following diagram, the forcible installation of democracy coupled with the recurring cycle of oppression among competing regimes illustrates the rise of ISIS as an *unintended consequence* of the U.S. intervention in Iraq.

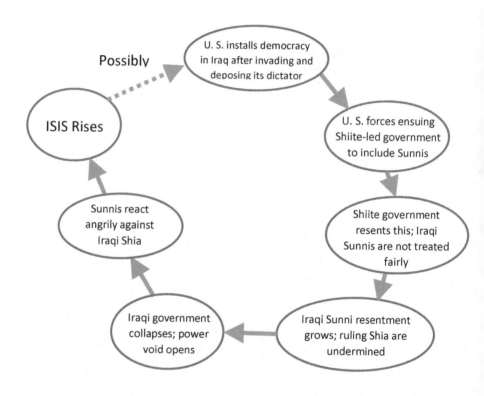

Figure VI-11. The Rise of ISIS.

It is clear from this CLD that this mistake could be repeated in the future if subsequent U. S. intervention is taken to defeat ISIS and impose democracy without understanding the potential unintentional consequences given the region's culture, history, and politics.

Causal Loop 4: Destruction of ISIS Infrastructure: One approach for accelerating the demise of ISIS is to deny it access to the resources and revenues needed to provide sustenance to its growing populace, which will result in a loss of internal support. As shown below, continued bombing of ISIS oil fields would weaken the ISIS military, reclaim some lost territory, and weaken support for ISIS among its constituents.

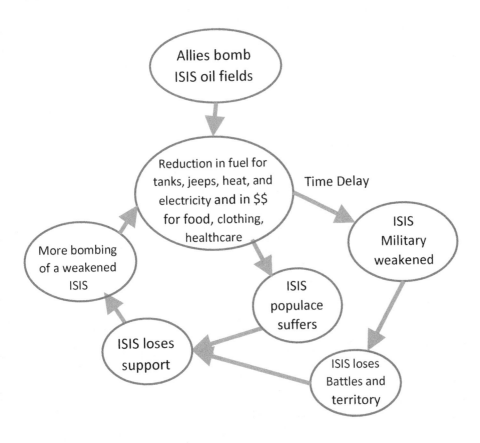

Figure VI-12. The Destruction of ISIS Infrastructure.

Causal Loop 5: Ransom for Hostages: An additional source of revenue for ISIS is the payment of ransom in exchange for the release of hostages. Success in generating funds from hostage-taking encourages the taking of more hostages.

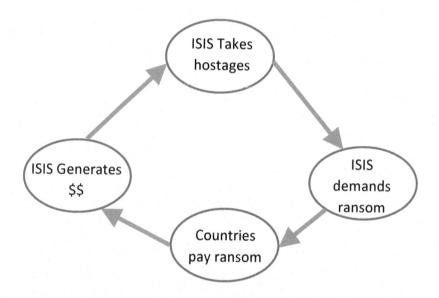

Figure VI-13. ISIS Revenue from Hostage Ransom.

It is clear from this CLD that the reinforcing feedback loop must be broken by refusing to pay ransom for hostages.

Step 4. **Discover the Structures.**

Step 5. **Discover the Mental Models.**

Several iceberg diagrams may be used to aid in both structure discovery and mental model identification. In Table VI-V, each row represents a different iceberg model:

Table VI-V. Iceberg Models Relevant to ISIS.

Iceberg Model Number	Mental Model	Resulting Structure	Pattern	Events
1	It is preferable to die a martyr (and ascend to paradise) than to continue the life I have been living.	ISIS, infrastructure for war, incentive for suicide bombings	War	Battles, suicide bombings
2	I will be 1 of the 5,000 ultimate survivors, if I am 1 of the 5,000 who follow the Koran most closely.	Religious and political structure of ISIS	Repeated Murders, rapes, beheadings, amputations, annual Jihad in the name of the Koran	Murders, rapes, beheadings, amputations, annual Jihad
3	If there will be 12 Caliphs before the end of time and we are on #8, then we had better get going!	The Caliphate, the propaganda, political, and social media efforts to engage the US and the rest of the world in war	Repeated outrageous provocations to expedite the Battle of Dabiq and the end of times	Live immolations, beheadings of innocents, enslavement, other sensational, provocative acts
4	The U.S. is a big, powerful bully that wants to eradicate Islam.	Political, Military, and Social structures that denigrate the U. S.	Increased opposition to U.S. intervention in foreign affairs, repeated anti-U.S. demonstrations and activities, attacks on U.S. embassies and military assets abroad	Anti-U.S. demonstrations and activities, attacks on U.S. embassies, military bases, ships and convoys

5	ISIS economic and government policies are more just, fairer, and more moral than my current government's.	Religious and political structure of ISIS; incentive structure for ISIS recruits	Recurring cycles of oppression and revolts between competing religious and political factions	Recruitment of ISIS fighters and civilians
6	Democracy is the best government and the US has the moral obligation to impose it.	The U. S. military and political machine	Repeated intervention in foreign affairs and forced installation of democratic governments	Intervention in countries we don't like and forced installation of democracies.
7	The US has a moral obligation to be the world's policeman.	The U. S. military and political machine	Repeated intervention in foreign affairs	Intervention in foreign affairs
8	Before I joined ISIS, my life meant nothing. Now, even if I die young, my life will have mattered.	ISIS, infrastructure for war, incentive for suicide bombings	War	Battles, suicide bombings
9	The sooner we destroy this world, the sooner we will be welcomed in paradise	Incentive to destroy as much of the world as possible, as soon as possible.	Repeated attempts to acquire nuclear weapons	Nuclear holocaust

Step 6. **Identify and Address Archetypes**. *The U. S. as World Policeman: The Addiction Archetype:* Although several archetypes are present (accidental adversaries, escalation, the rich get richer), the addiction archetype is

most prevalent. In this case, it is countries depending upon the U. S. to fight their battles, which ultimately de-values freedom and democracy because those countries don't need to fight battles and secure their freedom on their own. Freedom is devalued and underappreciated when it is just handed to a populace.

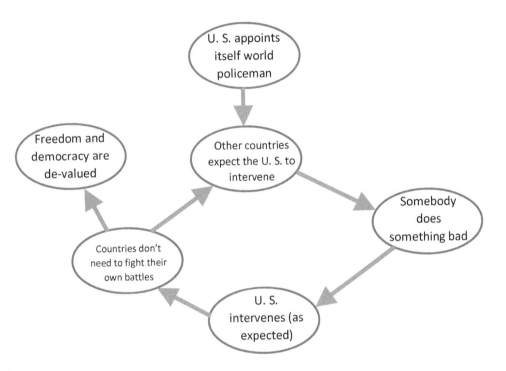

Figure VI-14. The Addiction Archetype.

Step 7. **Model (if appropriate).** Tools: Stock-and-Flow Diagrams, System Dynamics software.

    Step 7a. Develop the Model.

    Step 7b. Validate the Model.

    Step 7c. Identify Leverage Points.

    Step 7d. Optimize.

Modeling is useful for this situation. A simplified stock-and-flow diagram may be used to model the amount of resources and revenues ($$) needed as ISIS-controlled territory and population grow (Bronstein and Griffin, 2014). The diagram below was created using isee's iThink dynamic modeling software (model details are available from the authors). Territory Gain Rate, Revenues ($$) from Oil, and Per Person Costs of Food, Clothing, and Healthcare were set as independent variables in this model.

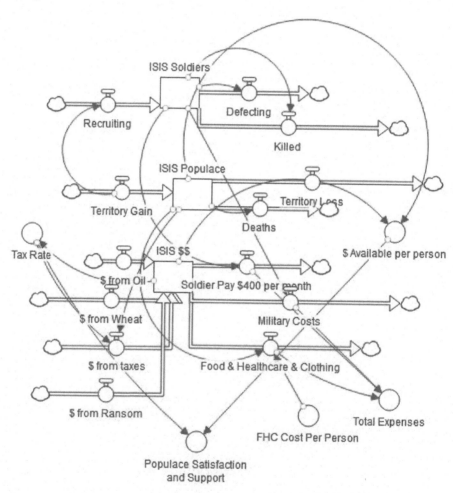

Figure VI-15. Dynamic Simulation Model of ISIS Revenue, Resources, Cash Reserves and Popular Support.

The following three figures are output graphs from the dynamic simulation, and illustrate a dramatic increase in expenses, a decrease in ISIS's cash reserves, and a dramatic decrease in popular support as ISIS gains territory and soldiers.

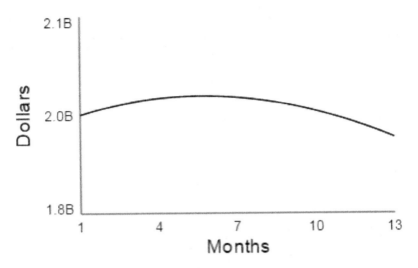

Figure VI-16. ISIS Cash Reserves versus Time.

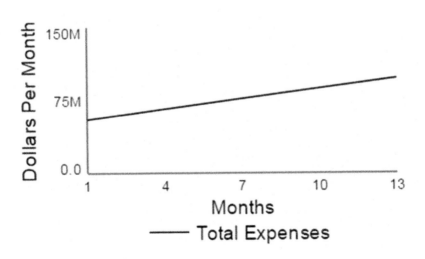

Figure VI-17. ISIS Expenses versus Time.

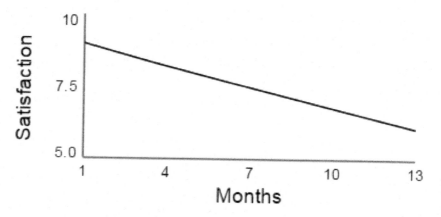

Figure VI-18. ISIS Popular Satisfaction and Support versus Time.

It is just about impossible to validate this model. Therefore, it is important to not use this dynamic simulation as a definitive quantitative representation, but only to elucidate cause-and-effect relationships, leverage points, and potential dynamic behaviors over time.

The model suggests that funding; rate of population gain via acquired territory; and food, clothing, and healthcare costs per person are key leverage points of the system. If the ISIS-controlled population increases faster than its revenues, then either ISIS's cash reserves or the services it provides to its people (or both) will decrease, resulting in loss of support. It is clear that destruction of ISIS's oil, wheat, and financial infrastructure while increasing the costs of food, clothing, and healthcare are keys to unravelling ISIS's popularity and support.

Step 8. **Determine the systemic root cause(s).**

The Five Why's and an Ishikawa diagram are helpful here. There are at least 3 questions to which the Five Why's may be applied:

> Why did ISIS rise?

> Why does ISIS appeal to some?

> Why does ISIS commit acts that seem to unite the rest of the world against it?

Applying the 5 why's to these questions requires some detail and may be found in Monat and Gannon (2015b).

Ishikawa Diagram:

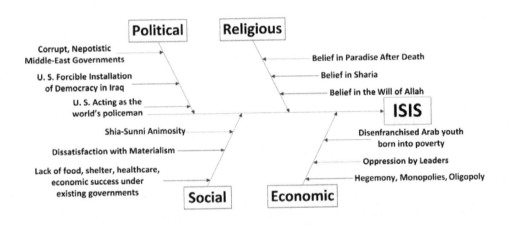

Figure VI-19. Ishikawa Diagram for ISIS

So what is the Root-Cause System? There are several cultures and belief structures that comprise the root cause system:

1. A culture of oppression, entitlement, nepotism, and corruption in some Middle-East countries.
2. A culture of helplessness, poverty, and despair among those countries' populations.
3. A philosophy/culture that the Unites States has both the right and the responsibility to act as the world's policeman and to forcibly install democracies.
4. A rationale that everything that happens is out of human control but is in the hands of a supreme being.
5. A mental model of a paradise-like afterlife that represents the only possibility of happiness and that world domination via whatever means necessary is the path there.

Step 9. **Make recommendations**.

1. The appeal of ISIS is not based upon high-level religious and spiritual ideals, but on basic human needs as articulated by Maslow (1943). Therefore attacking ISIS should focus on addressing *basic* (not philosophical, religious, or spiritual) human needs such as food, water, clothing, shelter, and health care.
2. The fight against ISIS should not be a military war but a socio-economic one fueled by social media.
3. The U. S. policy in the Middle East must change from forcibly installing democracies to one of an appreciation for the region's culture, history, and politics and one of incenting and rewarding Middle Eastern countries to become less corrupt, less coercive,

more accountable, and less based on nepotism and hereditary power.

4. The U. S. should stop acting as the World's Policeman.
5. The greatest threat to world peace is the evolution of Iran as a nuclear Caliphate. Therefore, this should be prevented by all means necessary (Greenfield, 2015).

Step 10. **Assess Improvement**.

It seems clear that Systems Thinking would yield vastly different approaches to geo-political problems than has linear thinking. The policy of advocating "bombing ISIS back to the stone age" which is advocated by some, is not a long-term solution as it does not address the root cause system that engenders organizations like ISIS.

Conclusion

Systems Thinking has great power in solving complex problems that are not solvable using conventional reductionist thinking. It can help to explain non-linear behaviors like market reactions to new product introductions or the spread of disease; to understand complex socio-economic problems such as the effects of charter schools or legalized gambling; and to understand the seemingly illogical behaviors of organizations and individuals.

Solving a problem using Systems Thinking begins with stating the problem or issue, defining the system, applying appropriate tools, and drawing conclusions. Those tools must be selected and the optimal sequence of application must be customized for each specific situation. Finally, the approach suggested in this handbook does not obviate the need for research at each step of the way: research into systemic structures, hidden mental models, equations governing dynamic behavior, and historic system behavior.

We hope that the tools and approach provided in this booklet facilitate the use of Systems Thinking in addressing issues of interest to you, whatever they may be.

References

American Society of Civil Engineers Review Panel, *The New Orleans Hurricane Protection System: What Went Wrong and Why*, American Society of Civil Engineers, 2007

Anderson, Virginia, and Johnson, Laura, *Systems Thinking Basics From Concepts to Causal Loops*, Pegasus Communications, Inc., Cambridge, 1997.

Attri, R., Dev, N., and Sharma, V., "Interpretive Structural Modelling (ISM) Approach: An Overview," Research Journal of Management Sciences **2**, 2013, 3-8.

Beckenkamp, Martin, "The Herd Moves? Emergence and Self-Organization in Collective Actors," Max Planck Institute for Research on Collective Goods, Bonn, 2006 http://www.coll.mpg.de.

Bellinger, Gene, "Archetypes: Interaction Structures of the Universe," 2004a, http://www.systems-thinking.org/arch/arch.htm

Bellinger, Gene, "Translating Systems Thinking Diagrams to Stock & Flow Diagrams," 2004b, http://www.systems-thinking.org/stsf/stsf.htm.

Bellinger, Gene, "Systems Thinking – A Disciplined Approach," 2004c, http://www.systems-thinking.org/stada/stada.htm.

Boardman, John and Sauser, Brian, *Systems Thinking: Coping With 21st Century Problems*, CRC Press, Boca Raton, 2008.

Bronstein, Scott, and Drew Griffin, "Self-Funded and Deep-Rooted: How ISIS Makes its Millions," CNN Investigations, October 7, 2014, http://www.cnn.com/2014/10/06/world/meast/isis-funding/

Bureau of Ocean Energy Management, Regulation and Enforcement (BOEMRE)/U.S. Coast Guard Joint Investigation Team (14 September 2011). "Deepwater Horizon Joint Investigation Team Releases Final Report" (Press release), U.S. Government.

Camazine, Scott, Jean-Louis Deneubourg, Nigel R. Franks, James Sneyd, Guy Theraulaz, & Eric Bonabeau, *Self-Organization in Biological Systems*, Princeton University Press, 2001.

Checkland, Peter, *Systems Thinking, Systems Practice,* John Wiley and Sons, New York, 1981.

Deming, W. Edwards, "Out of the Crisis," The MIT Press, Cambridge, MA, 1982.

Elmansy, Rafiq, "The Six Systems Thinking Steps to Solve Complex Problems," http://www.designorate.com/systems-thinking-steps-solve-complex-problems/, accessed 25 January 2017

Galley, Mark, "Think Reliability: Investigation Basics—The Systems Approach," Houston, 2014 http://www.investigationbasics.com/Systems-Approach.aspx .

Ganim, Sara, "Exclusive: Jerry Sandusky interview prompts long-ago victims to contact lawyer", *The Patriot-News*, November 17, 2011

Goodman, Michael, and Richard Karash, "Six Steps to Thinking Systemically," *Systems Thinker* **6** (2), Pegasus Communications, 1995

Goodman, Kemeny and Roberts, "The Language of Systems Thinking: 'Links' and 'Loops'," The Society of Organizational Learning, https://www.solonline.org/?page=Tool_LinksLoops&hhSearchTerms=%22systems+and+thinking%22.

Greenfield, Daniel, "Iran's Supreme Ayatollah Bashes US, Calls for Global Caliphate," *Frontpage Magazine*, June 6, 2015.

Gustin, Sam, "The Fatal Mistake That Doomed BlackBerry," Technology and Media, September 2013.

Hamid, Shadi, "Is There a Method to ISIS's Madness," Brookings Institute, Markaz, http://www.brookings.edu/blogs/markaz/posts/2015/11/24-isis-method-madness-hamid, November 24, 2015.

Hohler, Bob, "Inside the collapse of the 2011 Red Sox," Boston Globe Special Report, http://www.bostonglobe.com/sports/2011/10/11/red-sox-unity-dedication-dissolved-during-epic-late-season-collapse/KL4IT0morzpzJR0TsO1LsI/story.html, October 12, 2011.

isee Systems, Inc., 31 Old Etna Road, Lebanon, NH 03766, http://www.iseesystems.com/, 603-448-4990

Jackson, Rodney, and Som Ale, "Snow Leopards: Is Reintroduction the Best Option?" in Hayward, Matt, and Michael Somers, Eds., *Reintroduction of Top-Order Predators*, Blackwell Publishing Ltd, 2009, 165-186

Kim, Daniel H., *Introduction to Systems Thinking*, Pegasus Communications (now Leverage Networks Inc., www.leveragenetworks.com), 1999, ISBN 1-883823-34-X.

Lawson, Harold, *A Journey Through the Systems Landscape*, Volume 1 of the Systems Series, College Publications, London, 2010

Lendaris, George G., "Structural Modeling—A Tutorial Guide," ISEE Transactions on Systems, Man, and Cybernetics, SMC 10 (12), December 1980.

Maani, K. E., & Cavana, R. Y., *Systems Thinking, System Dynamic: Managing Change and Complexity* (2nd Ed.), Pearson: Prentice Hall, 2007.

Maslow, Abraham, "A Theory of Human Motivation," *Psychological Review*, **50** (4), 1943, 370-396.

McCants, William, *The ISIS Apocalypse: The History, Strategy, and Doomsday Vision of the Islamic State*, St. Martin Press, New York, 2015.

Meadows, Donella H., *Thinking in Systems: A Primer*, Chelsea Green Publishing, White River Junction, VT, 2008.

Monat, J. P., and Gannon, T.F., "What Is Systems Thinking? A Review of Selected Literature Plus Recommendations," *Am. J. of Systems Science*, **4**:2, 2015a

Monat, J. P., and Gannon, T.F., Using Systems Thinking to Analyze ISIS, *American Journal of Systems Science*, Vol. 4 No. 2, 2015b, pp. 36-49. doi: 10.5923/j.ajss.20150402.02.

Nagy Smith, Andrea, "What Was Polaroid Thinking?" Yale Insights, November, 2009.

National Commission on the BP Deepwater Horizon Oil Spill and Offshore Drilling (January 2011). "Deep Water: The Gulf Oil Disaster and the Future of Offshore Drilling," US Government.

Norman, Don, "Designing for People--Systems Thinking: A Product is More than the Product," *Interactions* **16** (5), Sept-Oct 2009

Richmond, Barry, *An Introduction to Systems Thinking with iThink*, isee Systems, 2004.

Robertson, Campbell, and John Schwartz, "Decade after Katrina pointing finger more firmly at Army Corps," *New York Times*, May 23, 2015.

Sauser, B., Building Systemic Diagrams; Systemigrams, Stevens Institute, https://www.stevens.edu/sse/sites/default/files/Systemigram_Overview.pdf, accessed 9 March 2015.

Senge, Peter, Kleiner, Art, Roberts, Charlotte, Ross, Richard, and Smith, Bryan, *The Fifth Discipline Fieldbook*,. Doubleday, New York, 1994.

Senge, Peter, *The Fifth Discipline*, Doubleday, New York, 1990; revised 2006.

Thompson, Loren, "Five Reasons The ISIS Fight Isn't About Islam," *Forbes*, February 26, 2015

Von Drehle, David, "The War on ISIS," *Time*, March 9, 2015.

Warfield, John N., Structuring Complex Systems (Monograph No. 4), Battelle Memorial Institute, Columbus OH, 1974.

Wikipedia, "Samsung," http://en.wikipedia.org/wiki/Samsung, accessed 5/5/2015.

Wood, Graeme, "What Isis Really Wants," *The Atlantic*, March2015, http://www.theatlantic.com/features/archive/2015/02/what-isis-really-wants/384980/

About the Authors

Jamie Monat is a Professor of Practice and Director at Worcester Polytechnic Institute, where he teaches courses in Operations Risk Management, Systems Thinking, System Optimization, Operations Management, Business Practices, and Project Management. Dr. Monat has both management and teaching experience in the medical device, separations, food & beverage, consulting, and environmental industries, having served as President of Harvard Clinical Technology, President of Business Growth Specialists, Inc., as Sr. Vice-President of Pall Corporation, and in a variety of positions for Koch Membrane Systems, Inc.

Dr. Monat's current research interests include applications of systems thinking, employee performance metrics, business applications of logistic regression, self-organization and emergence, project risk management, and operations risk analysis. He has a B.S. in Aerospace and Mechanical Sciences from Princeton, and an M.S. and Ph.D. in Environmental Engineering from Stanford. He has been at WPI since 2004 and may be reached at jmonat@wpi.edu.

Tom Gannon is a Professor of Practice in WPI's Systems Engineering program. He has over 45 years of experience in enterprise systems engineering, real-time control systems and information management systems. Before joining the WPI faculty on a full-time basis, Dr. Gannon was Director of Information Systems Engineering and Chief Engineer for the Technology and Innovation (T&I) Directorate of the Command and Control

Center (C2C) at the MITRE Corporation, where he was responsible for the formation and management of the Directorate's technology strategy, investment plans, and science and technology (S&T) program. Previously, he served as Director of the Corporate Technology Transfer Office at MITRE and held senior engineering management positions at Digital Equipment Corporation (DEC) and Bell Laboratories.

Dr. Gannon also served as a member of the Technical Advisory Boards and Board of Directors of several research consortia, including MCC, MCNC, SEMATECH and SRC, and as a member of the National Academy of Science Committee on International Trends in Computer Science and Technology. While at DEC, he also served as Chairman of the Technology Policy Committee of CSPP, a public policy forum established by the U.S. computer industry, and was responsible for directing the development of public policy positions on strategic technology issues which affected the global competitiveness of the U.S. computer industry.

Dr. Gannon holds a Ph.D. in Electrical Engineering and Computer Science from Stevens Institute of Technology, as well as an M.S. from Purdue University and a B.S. from the Illinois Institute of Technology, both in Electrical Engineering. He may be reached at tgannon@wpi.edu.

CPSIA information can be obtained
at www.ICGtesting.com
Printed in the USA
BVOW07s1301010817

490579BV00038B/173/P